D1186791

STANDARD GRADE | FOUNDATION | GENERAL

ENGLISH
2008-2012

SQA

BrightRED
PUBLISHING

First exam published in 2008.
Published by Bright Red Publishing Ltd, 6 Stafford Street, Edinburgh EH3 7AU
tel: 0131 220 5804 fax: 0131 220 6710 info@brightredpublishing.co.uk www.brightredpublishing.co.uk

ISBN 978-1-84948-243-1

A CIP Catalogue record for this book is available from the British Library.

Bright Red Publishing is grateful to the copyright holders, as credited on the final page of the Question Section, for permission to use their material. Every effort has been made to trace the copyright holders and to obtain their permission for the use of copyright material. Bright Red Publishing will be happy to receive information allowing us to rectify any error or omission in future editions.

STANDARD GRADE | FOUNDATION

2008
READING

[BLANK PAGE]

F

0860/401

NATIONAL
QUALIFICATIONS
2008

TUESDAY, 6 MAY
10.35 AM – 11.25 AM

ENGLISH
STANDARD GRADE
Foundation Level
Reading
Text

Read carefully the passage overleaf. It will help if you read it twice. When you have done so, answer the questions. Use the spaces provided in the Question/Answer booklet.

Home for Christmas

1   Christmas Eve was not a good day to hitch-hike. Billy had been at the motorway services for nearly five hours without a sniff of a lift. No-one had even slowed down to take a look at him. And the weather was lousy. At one point, he'd had to shelter from the rain next to some bins behind the petrol station. He'd dozed off, and there was another hour gone.

2   Now it was getting dark, and a fog was coming in. Cars drove by him as if he wasn't there. So much for Christmas spirit! It wasn't as though Billy had a big, off-putting bag either. All he carried was a small rucksack, which used to belong to his mum. It contained all his worldly goods, such as they were, and would fit beneath his legs in the smallest car.

3   Maybe he should cross the six-lane road, and try to hitch back to London, where he'd come from that morning. People said that you could get a bed and something to eat more easily at Christmas. But no. With Billy's luck, he'd probably get run over crossing the motorway.

4   Billy began to cough. He'd had this cold on and off for two months. Other homeless people told him that your body got used to the life, when you'd been living on the streets long enough. Maybe. He'd been sleeping rough for a year now. That was long enough for him to decide that it wasn't the life for him.

5   The fog was getting thicker. It was colder, too. When it got really dark, he'd wander into the café, warm up a bit. Billy had enough money left for a cup of coffee. That was, presuming they'd serve him. He looked a mess.

6   The rain started up again. Billy shivered. His jacket was supposed to be "shower-proof", but it was wet through. Puddles were forming around his feet. Suddenly, he saw a lorry, coming towards him from the direction of the petrol station. The lorry didn't have its lights on and was driving really close to the kerb. Instead of holding his thumb out, Billy took a step back. He didn't want to get splashed by the foul, oily water that lay on the road.

7   Still, the lorry seemed to be driving straight at him. Billy decided to get out of its way. But as he was about to make his move, the lorry turned its lights on, full beam. He couldn't see a thing. He stood there, frozen to the spot, like a rabbit dazzled by a poacher's torch, waiting to be shot.

8   The lorry stopped. One of its wheels was on the kerb, only centimetres from Billy's right foot. The passenger door opened. A deep voice spoke.

9   "You after a lift?"

10   It all felt wrong. Billy knew that. But it was raining hard now, and he had been there all day. He went up to the door and opened it a little farther.

11   "How far are you going?" the deep voice asked.

12   Billy still couldn't see the driver, only hear his harsh voice.

13   "I'm going to Scotland. To Gretna."

14   "I'm going that way myself. Get in."

15   Billy hesitated. He had learnt to walk away from threatening situations. But the man's accent was Scottish, like his, and he could take him all the way home—or, at least, to the place he used to call home.

16   Billy got into the cabin. He slid his bag beneath his feet and pulled on the seatbelt before looking at the driver.

17   "Thanks for stopping," he said. "It's pretty horrible out there."

18   The man said nothing. His thick hands reached for the gear stick. He began to accelerate onto the M1, towards the grim, frozen north.

19   In the half light of the lorry cabin, Billy looked at the driver. The man was in his late thirties, forty at most. He had short, dark hair. His eyes were set so deeply beneath his heavy eyebrows that Billy could barely make them out. His face was scarred. He was heavy set and wore a lumberjack shirt over shapeless jeans.

20   Billy hadn't done a lot of hitching, but he knew that there was an etiquette. The hitcher had to make conversation. It was your duty to entertain the driver, even if he didn't have a lot to say for himself. The driver had to concentrate on the driving, after all.

21   "I'm Billy," he said to the man, in his friendliest voice, "Billy Gates."

22   For a moment, he thought that the driver wasn't going to reply.

23   "Hank."

24   "Bad day to have to work, Christmas Eve."

25   Again, Hank didn't answer. Instead, he speeded up, until they were doing fifty. The fog was getting thicker and it felt too fast. Still, it wasn't Billy's place to say their speed was dangerous.

26   The silence was almost as threatening as the speed they were doing. There was a radio. Billy wondered whether he should suggest switching it on.

27   "Should I . . . ?"

28   Hank interrupted before Billy had formed the sentence.

29   "I don't like music."

30   The way he said it made Billy want to jump out of the cab, even though their speed was up to fifty-five and there was nothing but filthy fog outside. Instead, he began to say the first things that came into his mind.

31   "Do you know how many cars went by before you picked me up?"

32   Hank remained silent.

33   "A thousand at least."

34   Now that he'd starting talking, he couldn't stop.

35   "I think this time of year is a pain, really," Billy said. "You know what I mean? Everyone's expected to have a good time, so when you're not, somehow it seems a hundred times worse."

36   "Aye," said Hank. "I know that all right."

37   He began to drive even faster.

Adapted from a short story

[END OF PASSAGE]

[BLANK PAGE]

FOR OFFICIAL USE

F

Total Mark

0860/402

NATIONAL QUALIFICATIONS 2008

TUESDAY, 6 MAY 10.35 AM – 11.25 AM

ENGLISH STANDARD GRADE
Foundation Level
Reading
Questions

Fill in these boxes and read what is printed below.

Full name of centre

Town

Forename(s)

Surname

Date of birth
Day   Month   Year   Scottish candidate number   Number of seat

NB Before leaving the examination room you must give this booklet to the invigilator. If you do not, you may lose all the marks for this paper.

Mar

QUESTIONS

Write your answers in the spaces provided.

Look at Paragraphs 1 and 2.

1. **When** and **where** does the story begin?

   christmas Eve at the mother nucy services.

   2 1

2. ". . . not a good day to hitch-hike." (Paragraph 1)

   Give **two** pieces of evidence from Paragraph 1 which show this is true.

   (i) *no one slowed down to take a look at him*

   (ii) *the weather was lousy*

   2 1

3. Billy's situation becomes worse as it grows late.

   Write down two things from Paragraph 2 which add to his difficulties.

   (i) *cars drove past him as if he wasn't there*

   (ii) _____

   2 1

4. **Write down an expression** from Paragraph 2 which shows that drivers paid no attention to Billy.

   cars drove past him as if he wasn't there

   2 ∎

5. Billy is carrying a rucksack.

   Why would this **not** be a problem for drivers?

   it would fit beneath his legs in the smallest car

   2 ∎

PAG
TOT

Marks

6. Give **two** reasons why the rucksack might be important to Billy.

   it used to belongtohis mum and contained all his worldy goods

   2 | 1 | 0

Look at Paragraphs 3 to 5.

7. Billy thinks about crossing the road and returning to London.

   (*a*) Why does he consider doing this?

   people said that you could get a bed and something to eat more easily as chistmus

   2 | 1 | 0

   (*b*) Why does he decide **not** to?

   with his back he could get run over crossing the motorway

   2 | ■ | 0

8. Billy is in bad physical shape.

   (*a*) **Write down two ways** the writer shows us this.

   ~~he was in bad physical shape~~

   2 | 1 | 0

   (*b*) **Why** is Billy in such bad shape?

   an on and off cold, couldn't sleep well for a year

   2 | 1 | 0

9. Give **two** reasons why Billy plans to go into the café later.

   (i) *so he could warm up*

   (ii) _____

   2 | 1 | 0

10. **Write down an expression** which suggests he is a bit unsure about going into the café.

   they mite not serve his cothe looks a mess

   2 | ■ | 0

[Turn over

PAGE
TOTAL

Mar

Look at Paragraphs 6 and 7.

11. The weather is making Billy more and more miserable.

Write down three things which show this.

(i) his jaket was wet through

(ii) the rain started up again

(iii) _____   2 1

12. **Why** has the writer put inverted commas around the word "shower-proof"?

_____   2 ▪

13. When Billy **first** sees the lorry (Paragraph 6), which **two** things make it dangerous?

(i) _____

(ii) _____   2 1

14. ". . . like a rabbit dazzled by a poacher's torch, waiting to be shot." (Paragraph 7)

(*a*)   What technique is the writer using in this expression? Tick (✓) the correct box.

rhyme	
metaphor	
alliteration	
simile	

2 ▪

(*b*)   What **two** things does this expression suggest about Billy?

(i) _____

(ii) _____   2 1

PAG
TOT

Marks

Look at Paragraphs 8 to 18.

15. **Before** Billy gets into the lorry, how does the writer make the driver seem mysterious and threatening?

_____

2 1 0

16. "Billy hesitated." (Paragraph 15)

Give **two** reasons why he then decides to accept the lift after all.

(i) _____

(ii) _____

2 1 0

17. " . . . —or, at least, to the place he used to call home." (Paragraph 15)

How do you think Billy feels about his home in Scotland?

_____

2 ■ 0

18. " . . . the grim, frozen north." (Paragraph 18)

Explain why this is a good description of Billy's destination.

_____

2 1 0

Look at Paragraphs 19 and 20.

19. " . . . etiquette." (Paragraph 20)

Tick (✓) the box beside the best definition of "etiquette".

a conversation	
a gadget	
a way of behaving correctly	
a solution to a problem	

2 ■ 0

[Turn over for Questions 20 to 22 on *Page six*

PAGE
TOTAL

Mar

Look at Paragraphs 21 to 37.

20. Billy becomes more and more nervous.

   Write down three things about Hank's behaviour which make Billy feel like this.

   (i) _____

   (ii) _____

   (iii) _____   2 1

21. "Everyone's expected to have a good time . . ." (Paragraph 35)

   Why does this bother Billy?

   _____

   _____   2 1

Think about the passage as a whole.

22. Do you feel sorry for Billy?

   Tick (✓) **one** box.

   Yes [   ]

   No   [   ]

   Give **two** reasons from the passage to support your answer.

   (i) _____

   _____

   (ii) _____

   _____   2 1

[END OF QUESTION PAPER]

PA(
TO

FOR OFFICIAL USE

p2	
p3	
p4	
p5	
p6	
TOTAL MARK	

[BLANK PAGE]

[BLANK PAGE]

G

0860/403

NATIONAL
QUALIFICATIONS
2008

TUESDAY, 6 MAY
1.00 PM – 1.50 PM

ENGLISH
STANDARD GRADE
General Level
Reading
Text

Read carefully the passage overleaf. It will help if you read it twice. When you have done so, answer the questions. Use the spaces provided in the Question/Answer booklet.

Saddle the white horses

Thurso prepares to host its first professional surf tour, confirming Scotland's status as a world–class surfing destination.

1   It was the stickers that gave it away. Turning left on the A9 at Latheron in Caithness, you were suddenly faced with a sign that looked as though it had been defaced by advertising executives from surfing companies. Like a cairn on a mountain path, the big green board declaring Thurso to be 23 miles away told travelling bands of surfers that they'd taken the right turn-off and were nearly at their destination. Slapping another sticker on the sign was like laying another stone on the pile.

2   Thurso is about to enter surfing's big league.

3   It's hard to reconcile the popular tropical imagery of surfing with the town, a raw, exposed kind of place that enjoys little escape from the worst excesses of the Scottish climate. The Caithness coastline is peppered with surfing spots, but the jewel in the crown and the target for dedicated wave riders lies within spitting distance of Thurso town centre at a reef break called Thurso East. In the right conditions, the swell there rears up over kelp-covered slabs into a fast-moving, barrelling monster of a wave considered world class by those in the know.

4   Now Thurso East is the focus of a huge professional surfing tour. The week-long Highland Open marks the first time a World Qualifying Series (WQS) surfing competition has been held in Scotland. It will also be the furthest north a WQS tour has ever travelled, anywhere in the world.

5   Professional competitive surfing has two tours: the WQS and the World Championship Tour (WCT). The WCT is the premier division, with the WQS being used as a platform for professionals to move up into the big time. Around 160 up-and-coming wave riders are expected to take part in the Thurso event. Prize money of $100,000 (£57,000) is up for grabs, along with vital tour points.

6   "Travelling and exploring new places is part of the whole surfing culture," says Bernhard Ritzer, the Highland Open event manager. "We've had so much feedback from surfers from Australia and Brazil who want to go. They see it as an adventure and as something new. We did a photo trip there last year with some of our team riders and they were impressed. They're excited about it—although it will still be a shock because I don't think they know how cold and harsh it can be."

7   "Thurso is one of the best waves in Europe, if not the world," he says. "Most people don't even know it, and it's just so good. It doesn't always have to be sunny, warm and tropical. It can also be cold, rough and hard.

8   "The idea is to have a contrast to the summer events in the tropical islands. We also have something in the north to show that this is part of surfing. Very often on the WQS tour the waves aren't that good, but here they are expecting big reef break waves and they like to surf those."

9   Surfers generally guard their local breaks jealously. It's considered essential to keep your mouth shut about your "secret spot", in case you find it overrun with visitors. So, economic benefits to Thurso aside, some local surfers were a little concerned about an event on this scale descending on their area. WQS representatives met with these surfers to address their concerns and feel that they've pretty much got everyone on board. WQS is also paying for improvements to the car parking area near the Thurso East break.

10   "We're concerned to get the locals involved," says Ritzer. "We want to keep them happy and don't want to look too commercial, coming in with a big event machine. We need them to help organise local stuff. You always have some individuals who will boycott everything, but we understand that most of them are positive."

11   Andy Bain probably knows the break at Thurso East better than anyone, although he'll be watching the competition from the shoreline. Bain, who runs Thurso Surf, has been surfing the reef there for 17 years and is eagerly anticipating the arrival of the Highland Open. He's aware of the concerns and the possible exposure of his home break, but doesn't anticipate a negative impact.

12   "From the surf school side of things it's good because it'll generate business for us," says Bain, 33. "As a local surfer, it's kind of like closure for me to have this competition. To say the world has now recognised Thurso as a top surfing destination makes me feel proud. A lot of people say it's going to get crowded and exposed, but with it being a cold destination I don't think it's going to be that bad."

13   For professional surfer Adam Robertson from Victoria, Australia, the trip to Thurso will be something of a journey into the unknown. "This will be the first time I've ever been to Scotland," says Robertson, who has competed on the WQS tour for the past three years. "We're all a bit worried about how cold it's going to be. Apart from that we're pretty excited because it's a place we've never been."

14   Robertson, 23, who has been surfing since he was four, criss-crosses the globe with his fellow WQS competitors in pursuit of the best waves and a place on the coveted WCT tour. He may as well be going to surf on the moon for all he knows about Thurso East, but that's part of the appeal.

15   "We follow the surf around all year and go to a lot of different places, but Scotland's somewhere probably none of us have been to," he says. "That for me was a big part of wanting to go, to see the place. As a professional surfer, you've got to live out of your bag a lot, travelling around with long stints away from home, but when you perform well in the event or get some really good waves, it makes it all worth it.

16   "I feel pretty good and I'm hoping to do well," he adds. "Everyone who does the tour is feeling good too, so it should be a great event. It'll be interesting to see what the waves are like."

17   Competitors will be scored by a team of eight international judges on the length of their ride, the difficulty of moves and how they connect it all together. Waves are scored on a one to ten scale, with ten a perfect ride, and the final scores are based on each surfer's two highest-scoring waves.

18   "These events raise the profile of locations, create investment in areas and hopefully provide opportunities for young surfers coming through to grow and compete at world-class levels," says Dave Reed, contest director for the WQS event. "It's a great way to say we've got some of the best waves in the world."

Adapted from a magazine article

[END OF PASSAGE]

[BLANK PAGE]

FOR OFFICIAL USE

Total
Mark

G

0860/404

NATIONAL
QUALIFICATIONS
2008

TUESDAY, 6 MAY
1.00 PM – 1.50 PM

ENGLISH
STANDARD GRADE
General Level
Reading
Questions

Fill in these boxes and read what is printed below.

Full name of centre

Town

Forename(s)

Surname

Date of birth
Day Month Year

Scottish candidate number

Number of seat

**NB Before leaving the examination room you must give this booklet to the invigilator.
If you do not, you may lose all the marks for this paper.**

Mark

QUESTIONS

Write your answers in the spaces provided.

Look at Paragraphs 1 to 3.

1. (*a*)   What had been added to the road sign in Caithness?

_____   2

(*b*)   Write down **two** things the surfers would know when they saw this road sign.

_____

_____   2   1

2. "Thurso is about to enter surfing's big league." (Paragraph 2)

How does the writer make this statement stand out?

_____   2

3. Thurso is different from the popular image of a surfing location.

(*a*)   **In your own words**, describe the popular image of a surfing location.

_____   2

(*b*)   **Write down an expression** showing how Thurso is different.

_____   2

4. What do the words "jewel in the crown" (Paragraph 3) suggest about Thurso East?

_____   2

5. ". . . a fast-moving, barrelling monster . . ." (Paragraph 3)

Explain fully why this is an effective description of the wave.

_____

_____   2   1

PAG
TOT.

Marks

Look at Paragraphs 4 and 5.

6. In which **two** ways is the Highland Open different from other WQS surfing competitions?

    (i) _____

    (ii) _____   2 | 1 | 0

7. **In your own words**, explain the difference between the two professional surfing tours.

    WCT _____

    WQS _____   2 | 1 | 0

8. Which **two** benefits will the winner of the competition gain?

    (i) _____

    (ii) _____   2 | 1 | 0

Look at Paragraphs 6 to 8.

9. Give **three** reasons why, according to Bernhard Ritzer, surfers will want to visit Thurso.

    (i) _____

    (ii) _____

    (iii) _____   2 | 1 | 0

10. According to Ritzer, what will surprise the surfers?

    _____   2 | ■ | 0

[Turn over

PAGE
TOTAL

Mar

11. Thurso can offer something which many other surfing locations cannot.

What is this?

_____   2 ■

Look at Paragraphs 9 and 10.

12. "Surfers generally guard their local breaks . . . " (Paragraph 9)

In your own words, explain why surfers do this.

_____   2 1

13. What **style** of language is used in the expression "keep your mouth shut" (Paragraph 9)?

_____   2 ■

14. Which **two key** things have WQS representatives done to gain support?

(i) _____

(ii) _____   2 1

15. The WQS representatives feel that "they've pretty much got everyone on board." (Paragraph 9)

Write down an expression from Paragraph 10 which continues this idea.

_____   2 ■

16. **Write down a single word** from this section meaning "refuse to support or take part".

```
┌──────────────────────────┐
│                          │
│                          │
└──────────────────────────┘
```

2 ■

Marks

Look at Paragraphs 11 to 18.

17. (a) How does local surfer Andy Bain feel about the competition?

Tick (✓) the best answer.

very negative and angry	
quite pleased but worried	
excited and not really anxious	

2 ■ 0

(b) **Write down an expression** to support your chosen answer.

_____

2 ■ 0

18. "He may as well be going to surf on the moon . . . " (Paragraph 14)

What does this comparison suggest about Thurso?

_____

2 ■ 0

19. In Paragraph 15, Australian Adam Robertson describes his life as a professional surfer.

In your own words, sum up the **negative** and **positive** aspects of his life.

(a) **negative:** _____

_____

2 1 0

(b) **positive:** _____

_____

2 1 0

20. What **three** elements of the surfers' performance are judged?

(i) _____

(ii) _____

(iii) _____

2 1 0

[Turn over

PAGE
TOTAL

Mar

Think about the passage as a whole.

21.   (i) What do you think is the main purpose of this passage?

Tick (✓) **one** box.

to tell the reader some amusing stories about surfing	
to inform the reader about a surfing competition in Scotland	
to argue against holding a surfing competition in Scotland	

(ii) Give a reason to support your answer.

_____

_____   2 1

[END OF QUESTION PAPER]

PAC
TOT

FOR OFFICIAL USE

p2	
p3	
p4	
p5	
p6	
TOTAL MARK	

FOR OFFICIAL USE

[BLANK PAGE]

STANDARD GRADE | FOUNDATION

2009
READING

[BLANK PAGE]

F

0860/401

NATIONAL
QUALIFICATIONS
2009

FRIDAY, 8 MAY
10.35 AM – 11.25 AM

ENGLISH
STANDARD GRADE
Foundation Level
Reading
Text

Read carefully the passage overleaf. It will help if you read it twice. When you have done so, answer the questions. Use the spaces provided in the Question/Answer booklet.

In the following passage, Tom, a boy who has just arrived in Australia, is taken on a trip by his new friends, Sam and Greg.

1   They camped much later that afternoon on top of a low cliff above the river. The river was lined with trees. They reminded Tom of children's drawings with their square-shaped trunks and stubby little branches.

2   The river glided over polished white boulders. There were lily pads a metre wide with huge purple flowers at their centre. The nearest pads were about thirty metres away. Bright green ferns grew amongst the cracks in the rocky sides.

3   Tom looked round to see what the others were doing then scrambled down to the river's edge. There was a wide sandy beach on the opposite bank. Tom studied it. It wouldn't take any time to swim there and back and he wanted a swim very badly. He was sweat-stained and tired. There was sand in his hair, under his fingernails and inside his shorts.

4   He slipped off his shoes and stood ankle deep in the water. He closed his eyes and let the sensation engulf him. The water felt like silk. He took a deep breath and slowly let it out. The stress of the day began to disappear. He could stay here for ever, he decided. A bird shrilled from a nearby bush. He waded further out.

5   "Hey!" Sam's shout interrupted his sense of well-being. "Tom! Get back! What the heck you doing!" He came scrambling down the rocks in a flurry of arms and legs. He grabbed Tom's arm and dragged him away.

6   "You want to see your mother again?" he hissed, putting his face into Tom's. "You want to get me into big trouble?" He scowled at Tom. "You think you know better than me?"

7   "Hey look! I'm sorry . . ." began Tom.

8   "Me too," Sam snapped. Then he shook his head. "It's my fault. I forgot to tell you about crocodiles. Saltwater crocodiles. The scariest in the world. I'm a stupid man."

9   It was Tom's turn to reassure. "Don't worry," he said. "I had a really good look before I came down. There was nothing there. I promise you."

10   Sam cleared his throat and spat on to the sand. "See those lily pads?" he pointed, grabbing Tom's arm. "The crocs hide under there and watch. They don't miss a trick. They can stay there all day, waiting. Then an animal like you comes along and thinks everything is safe." He clapped his hands together. "Big mistake!"

11   He shook his finger at Tom. "Want to know how bad it is?" he said. "Most families round here have someone taken by a croc every year."

12   Tom's mouth dropped.

13   Sam shrugged. "That's how it goes," he said. "Think you can run fast?" he asked and without waiting for Tom's reply added, "No man alive can outrun a crocodile. They can do twenty miles an hour over fifty metres." He grinned suddenly at Tom. "You get chased by a six-metre-long saltwater with its jaws open, it's time to say goodbye, my friend. Ain't nothing that can help you then."

14   "Hey! You guys!" came Greg's voice from above. "Come and give us a hand! I'm not making camp on my own!"

15   They hurried back to the vehicle. Greg had already unpacked a small mound of stores. They all set to and very quickly had put up the tent, two camp beds and got the food organised.

16   "Doesn't Sam have a bed?" Tom asked, looking round inside the tent.

17   Sam shook his head. "Always sleep on the ground."

18   "Keeps the snakes from coming inside!" Greg laughed.

19   Later, Tom went off with Sam to collect wood for the camp fire. There was plenty lying around and all of it tinder dry. Tom worked steadily picking up branches and dragging them into a pile. He stopped under a tree and took a breather. He looked up and was puzzled to see a number of triangular-shaped leaves hanging down from a branch.

20   Tom stared at them. He had never seen leaves this shape or size before. Then he noticed that they weren't just a single leaf but several, all joined together. Intrigued, he picked up a long thin stick and tapped the nearest one.

21   Seconds later the whole branch was boiling over with enraged ants. But ants of a kind he had never seen before. Bright green ants in their thousands swarmed over every inch of the bark. Some fell on to his arm and he yelled in surprise. It felt as if a dozen red-hot injection needles had suddenly been thrust through his skin. He ran, slapping at them. Sam thought it a great joke and picked a whole lot more from Tom's hair.

22   "They're bad, those things," Greg remarked, when they got back to camp. "Probably kill you if enough got hold of you. Bit stupid of you annoying 'em. This isn't a park in London, you know."

23   Tom said nothing. Greg as usual was right. Then, while Sam went off to check the vehicle, he helped Greg build the fire. Tom watched Greg dig a shallow hole. "Aren't we going to have a bonfire?" Tom asked.

24   Greg stared at him. "Take a look around," he advised. "If this place catches fire we're all dead men. Ever seen a bush fire before?"

25   Tom thought of the muddy paths that criss-crossed the woods back home. He shook his head. How could he?

26   "You get a wall of fire metres high in a couple of minutes," Greg told him. "Goes across the ground faster than you can drive. This way, we keep the sparks down. In the morning, you just fill it back in with earth. Simple and safe."

27   Greg opened a packet of firelighters and pulled one out. Tom saw they were the same ones that his grandmother used back home. He was amused. "Why aren't you rubbing sticks together or something?" he joked.

28   Greg looked up at him, puzzled. "Don't be daft," he said. "What do you think matches are for?"

Adapted from the novel "Crocodile River" by Geoffrey Malone

[END OF PASSAGE]

[BLANK PAGE]

FOR OFFICIAL USE

F

Total
Mark

0860/402

NATIONAL
QUALIFICATIONS
2009

FRIDAY, 8 MAY
10.35 AM – 11.25 AM

ENGLISH
STANDARD GRADE
Foundation Level
Reading
Questions

Fill in these boxes and read what is printed below.

Full name of centre

Town

Forename(s)

Surname

Date of birth
Day Month Year

Scottish candidate number

Number of seat

**NB Before leaving the examination room you must give this booklet to the invigilator.
If you do not, you may lose all the marks for this paper.**

Mark

QUESTIONS

Write your answers in the spaces provided.

Look at Paragraphs 1 and 2.

1. What kind of trip were Tom and his friends on?

   _____   2 ■

2. The river was moving smoothly. Write down **one** word from Paragraph 2 which shows this.

   _____   2 ■

3. In the countryside around Tom, things were **large** and **colourful**. Write down **one** example of something large and **one** example of something colourful around Tom.

   large: _____

   colourful: _____   2 1

Look at Paragraphs 3 to 6.

4. Give **three** reasons why Tom "wanted a swim very badly". (Paragraph 3)

   (i) _____

   (ii) _____

   (iii) _____   2 1

Marks

5. "The water felt like silk." (Paragraph 4)

    (*a*) What technique is the writer using in this expression? Tick (✓) the correct box.

metaphor	
simile	
alliteration	
contrast	

    2 ■ 0

    (*b*) What does this expression suggest about how the water felt?

    _____

    2 ■ 0

6. Why did Tom feel he "could stay here for ever"? (Paragraph 4)

    _____

    2 ■ 0

7. What stopped Tom from enjoying the water?

    _____

    2 1 0

8. Sam was clearly angry with Tom.

    Write down **one thing he did to Tom** and **one thing he said** which clearly showed he was angry.

    (i) _____

    (ii) _____

    2 1 0

    [Turn over

PAGE
TOTAL

Mar

Look at Paragraphs 7 to 9.

9. Why did Sam call himself "a stupid man"? (Paragraph 8)

_____

2   1

10. Explain fully why Tom thought the water was safe.

_____

_____

2   1

Look at Paragraphs 10 to 13.

11. In Paragraph 10, Sam explained that crocodiles are good hunters.

Write down **two** things from Paragraph 10 which show they are good hunters.

(i) _____

(ii) _____

2   1

12. Why did Tom's mouth drop? (Paragraph 12)

_____

2   ■

13. Write down **two** pieces of evidence from Paragraph 13 which show how fast a crocodile can move.

(i) _____

(ii) _____

2   1

Look at Paragraphs 15 to 17.

14. Tom thinks something is missing from the tent. **What** does he think is missing and **why** is it not needed?

_____

_____

2   1

PAG
TOT

Marks

Look at Paragraphs 19 and 20.

15. Tom was "intrigued" by the strange leaves. (Paragraph 20)

    What does this mean he wanted to do? Tick (✓) the best answer.

eat them	
count them	
destroy them	
learn about them	

2 ■ 0

Look at Paragraph 21.

16. Explain why "boiling over" is a good way to describe the ants.

    _____

    _____

2 ■ 0

17. When the ants landed on Tom, it felt like "a dozen red-hot injection needles".
    Give **two** reasons why it felt like this.

    (i) _____

    (ii) _____

2 1 0

18. How do we know that Sam was not very worried about the ant attack?

    _____

2 ■ 0

Look at Paragraphs 22 to 27.

19. What did Greg mean when he said "This isn't a park in London"? (Paragraph 22)

    _____

2 ■ 0

[Turn over for Questions 20 to 24 on *Page six*

PAGE
TOTAL

Mar

20. What did Greg do to make sure their fire was safe?

_____   2 ■

21. Explain fully why the boys had to be careful about the fire.

_____

_____   2 1

22. "Simple and safe." (Paragraph 26)

What makes this expression stand out?

_____   2 ■

23. Why was Tom "amused" when he saw the firelighters? (Paragraph 27)

_____

_____   2 1

Think about the passage as a whole.

24. Tick (✓) the word which you feel best sums up Tom's experience of camping.

terrifying	
exciting	
embarrassing	

Give **two** pieces of evidence from the passage to support your answer.

(i) _____

(ii) _____   2 1

[END OF QUESTION PAPER]

PAG
TOT

FOR OFFICIAL USE

p2	
p3	
p4	
p5	
p6	
TOTAL MARK	

[BLANK PAGE]

[BLANK PAGE]

G

0860/403

| NATIONAL QUALIFICATIONS 2009 | FRIDAY, 8 MAY 1.00 PM – 1.50 PM | ENGLISH STANDARD GRADE General Level Reading Text |

Read carefully the passage overleaf. It will help if you read it twice. When you have done so, answer the questions. Use the spaces provided in the Question/Answer booklet.

In the following passage, Alice, the main character, is spending the summer working in France.

1   Alice notices a fly on the underside of her arm.

2   Insects are an occupational hazard at a dig, and for some reason there are more flies higher up the mountain where she is working than at the main excavation site lower down.

3   Her concentration broken, Alice stands up and stretches. She unscrews the top of her water bottle. It's warm, but she's too thirsty to care and drinks it down in great gulps. Below, the heat haze shimmers above the dented tarmac of the road. Above her, the sky is an endless blue.

4   It's her first time in the Pyrenees, although she feels very much at home. In the main camp on the lower slopes, Alice can see her colleagues standing under the big canvas awning. She's surprised they've stopped already. It's early in the day to be taking a break, but then the whole team is a bit demoralised. It's hard work: the digging, scraping, cataloguing, recording, and so far they've turned up little to justify their efforts. They've come across only a few fragments of early medieval pots and bowls, and a couple of arrowheads.

5   Alice is tempted to go down and join her colleagues. Her calves are already aching from squatting. The muscles in her shoulders are tense. But she knows that if she stops now, she'll lose her momentum.

6   Hopefully, her luck's about to change. Earlier, she'd noticed something glinting beneath a large boulder, propped against the side of the mountain, almost as if it had been placed there by a giant hand. Although she can't make out what the object is, even how big it is, she's been digging all morning and she doesn't think it will be much longer before she can reach it.

7   She knows she should fetch someone. Alice is not a trained archaeologist, just a volunteer. But it's her last day on site and she wants to prove herself. If she goes back down to the main camp now and admits she's on to something, everybody will want to be involved, and it will no longer be her discovery.

8   In the days and weeks to come, Alice will look back to this moment. She will wonder at how different things might have been had she made the choice to go and not to stay. If she had played by the rules.

9   She drains the last drop of water from the bottle and tosses it into her rucksack. For the next hour or so, as the sun climbs higher in the sky and the temperature rises, Alice carries on working. The only sounds are the scrape of metal on rock, the whine of insects and the occasional buzz of a light aircraft in the distance.

10   Alice kneels down on the ground and leans her cheek and shoulder against the rock for support. Then, with a flutter of excitement, she pushes her fingers deep into the dark earth. Straight away, she knows she's got something worth finding. It is smooth to the touch, metal not stone. Grasping it firmly and telling herself not to expect too much, slowly, slowly she eases the object out into the light.

11   The rich, cloying smell of wet soil fills her nose and throat, although she barely notices. She is already lost in the past, captivated by the piece of history she cradles in the palms of her hands. It is a heavy, round buckle, speckled black and green with age and from its long burial.

12   Alice is so absorbed that she doesn't notice the boulder shifting on its base. Then something makes her look up. For a split second, the world seems to hang suspended, out of space, out of time. She is mesmerised by the ancient slab of stone as it sways and tilts, and then gracefully begins to fall towards her. At the very last moment, the light fractures. The spell is broken. Alice throws herself out of the way, half tumbling, half slithering sideways, just in time to avoid being crushed. The boulder hits the ground with a dull thud, sending up a cloud of pale brown dust, then rolls over and over, as if in slow motion, until it comes to rest further down the mountain.

13   Alice clutches desperately at the bushes and scrub to stop herself slipping any further. For a moment she lies sprawled in the dirt, dizzy and disorientated. As it sinks in how very close she came to being crushed, she turns cold. Takes a deep breath. Waits for the world to stop spinning.

14   Gradually, the pounding in her head dies away. The sickness in her stomach settles and everything starts to return to normal, enough for her to sit up and take stock. Her knees are grazed and streaked with blood and she's knocked her wrist where she landed awkwardly, still clutching the buckle in her hand to protect it, but basically she's escaped with no more than a few cuts and bruises.

15   She gets to her feet and dusts herself down. She raises her hand, is about to call out to attract someone's attention when she notices that there's a narrow opening visible in the side of the mountain where the boulder had been standing. Like a doorway cut into the rock.

16   She hesitates. Alice knows she should get somebody to come with her. It is stupid, possibly even dangerous, to go in on her own without any sort of back-up. She knows all the things that can go wrong. But something is drawing her in. It feels personal. It's her discovery.

17   She climbs back up. There is a dip in the ground at the mouth of the cave, where the stone had stood guard. The damp earth is alive with the frantic writhing of worms and beetles exposed suddenly to the light and heat after so long. Her cap lies on the ground where it fell. Her trowel is there too, just where she left it.

18   Alice peers into the darkness. The opening is no more than five feet high and about three feet wide and the edges are irregular and rough. It seems to be natural rather than man-made.

19   Slowly, her eyes become accustomed to the gloom. Velvet black gives way to charcoal grey and she sees that she is looking into a long, narrow tunnel.

20   Squeezing the buckle tightly in her hand, she takes a deep breath and steps forward into the passageway. Straight away, the smell of long-hidden, underground air surrounds her, filling her mouth and throat and lungs. It's cool and damp, not the dry, poisonous gases of a sealed cave she's been warned about, so she guesses there must be some source of fresh air.

21   Feeling nervous and slightly guilty, Alice wraps the buckle in a handkerchief and pushes it into her pocket, then cautiously steps forward.

22   As she moves further in, she feels the chill air curl around her bare legs and arms like a cat. She is walking downhill. She can feel the ground sloping away beneath her feet, uneven and gritty. The scrunch of the stones and gravel is loud in the confined, hushed space. She is aware of the daylight getting fainter and fainter at her back, the further and deeper she goes.

23   Abruptly, she does not want to go on.

Adapted from the novel "Labyrinth" by Kate Mosse

[END OF PASSAGE]

[BLANK PAGE]

FOR OFFICIAL USE

Total
Mark

0860/404

NATIONAL
QUALIFICATIONS
2009

FRIDAY, 8 MAY
1.00 PM – 1.50 PM

ENGLISH
STANDARD GRADE
General Level
Reading
Questions

G

Fill in these boxes and read what is printed below.

Full name of centre

Town

Forename(s)

Surname

Date of birth
Day Month Year

Scottish candidate number

Number of seat

**NB Before leaving the examination room you must give this booklet to the invigilator.
If you do not, you may lose all the marks for this paper.**

SA 0860/404 6/63420

Mar

QUESTIONS

Write your answers in the spaces provided.

Look at Paragraphs 1 and 2.

1. What activity is Alice involved in?

   _____   2 ■

2. "Insects are an occupational hazard . . . " (Paragraph 2)

   Explain **in your own words** what this means.

   _____

   _____   2 1

Look at Paragraphs 3 to 5.

3. Write down **three** things the writer tells us in Paragraph 3 which show that it is a hot day.

   (i) _____

   (ii) _____

   (iii) _____   2 1

4. How does the writer emphasise that "It's hard work"? (Paragraph 4)

   (*a*) by sentence structure

   _____   2 ■

   (*b*) by word choice

   _____   2 ■

5. Write down an expression from the passage which suggests the hard work has not been worth it so far.

   _____   2 ■

PAG
TOT

Marks

6. "Alice is tempted to go down and join her colleagues." (Paragraph 5)

Give **two** reasons why she is tempted to do this.

(i) _____

(ii) _____   2 1 0

Look at Paragraph 7.

7. Tick (✓) the appropriate box to show whether the following statements about Alice are True, False or Cannot Tell from the passage.

	True	False	Cannot Tell			
She wants to show that she can do the job herself.				2	■	0
She does not like her colleagues.				2	■	0
She wants to share her discovery.				2	■	0

Look at Paragraph 10.

8. In Paragraph 10, the writer shows Alice's **feelings** and **thoughts** as she pushes her hand into the soil.

(*a*) **Write down one** expression which shows her **feelings** at this point.

_____   2 ■ 0

(*b*) **Write down one** expression which shows her **thoughts** at this point.

_____   2 ■ 0

9. Why does the writer repeat the word "slowly" in Paragraph 10?

_____   2 ■ 0

[Turn over

PAGE TOTAL

Mar

Look at Paragraphs 11 and 12.

10. Alice is "captivated" by the buckle she has found. (Paragraph 11)

Write down **one** other word from the next paragraph (Paragraph 12) which **also** shows how interested she is in the buckle.

2 ■

11. Give **two** reasons why Alice does not move out of the way of the boulder until the last moment.

(i) _____

(ii) _____

2   1

12. Explain carefully what is surprising about the word "gracefully" in Paragraph 12.

_____

2   1

Look at Paragraphs 13 to 16.

13. " . . . dirt, dizzy and disorientated." (Paragraph 13)

Identify the **technique** used here.

_____

2 ■

14. **In your own words**, explain why Alice "turns cold". (Paragraph 13)

_____

_____

2   1

15. Why do you think Alice does **not** "call out to attract someone's attention"? (Paragraph 15)

_____

_____

2   1

PAC
TOT

Marks

Look at Paragraphs 17 to 19.

16. ". . . the stone had stood guard." (Paragraph 17)

   Give **two** reasons why this expression is appropriate.

   (i) _____

   (ii) _____   2 1 0

17. "Slowly, her eyes become accustomed to the gloom." (Paragraph 19)

   Explain how the writer develops this idea in the next sentence.

   _____

   _____   2 1 0

Look at Paragraph 21 to the end of the passage.

18. As Alice steps into the tunnel, she experiences **two** feelings. **In your own words**, explain what these **two** feelings are.

   (i) _____

   (ii) _____   2 1 0

19. "Abruptly, she does not want to go on." (Paragraph 23)

   Give **two** reasons why this is an effective ending to the passage.

   (i) _____

   (ii) _____   2 1 0

[Turn over

PAGE
TOTAL

Mar

Think about the passage as a whole.

20. The writer has written this story in the present tense.

Why do you think the writer has done this?

_____

2

21. What do you think will happen next in the story?

Tick (✓) the answer which you think is most likely.

Alice will return to her colleagues.	
Alice will go further into the cave and make an exciting discovery.	
Alice will be trapped in the cave.	

Give **two** pieces of evidence from the passage to support your answer.

(i) _____

(ii) _____

2 **1**

[END OF QUESTION PAPER]

PA(
TO1

FOR OFFICIAL USE

[0860/404]

p2	
p3	
p4	
p5	
p6	
TOTAL MARK	

FOR OFFICIAL USE

[BLANK PAGE]

STANDARD GRADE | FOUNDATION

2010
READING

[BLANK PAGE]

F

0860/401

NATIONAL
QUALIFICATIONS
2010

THURSDAY, 29 APRIL
10.35 AM – 11.25 AM

ENGLISH
STANDARD GRADE
Foundation Level
Reading
Text

Read carefully the passage overleaf. It will help if you read it twice. When you have done so, answer the questions. Use the spaces provided in the Question/Answer booklet.

In the following passage, the main character Theo has a frightening experience.

1   About the time that Theo Dove turned thirteen, he became ill, and had to spend several weeks in bed. The holidays were due, so he did not miss much school. This pleased Theo, as he enjoyed school, but it was a boring, disagreeable time. After the first two weeks he was not exactly ill, and not exactly well. The fever and aches and wobbliness were bad enough, but worse was the way he felt, as if a damp grey curtain had been dropped between him and the world.

2   This way of feeling was not Theo's line at all. He was a sharp, stringy person, always on the go, interested in most things, and ready to do something about them. When he was small he had overheard his mother telling someone that he was a fearless little boy. At the time he hadn't been quite sure how to think of himself, and he had been much taken by the description. It had been no sweat living up to it ever since. But after the illness, he didn't much care for anything. Not even the house-moving, that had happened in his fourth week of being sick. Then the Doves left Parramatta, and moved to a brand-new housing development east of the Nepean River. It was a giant leap forward for the family because Cheapies, the supermarket people for whom Mr Dove worked, had opened a branch there, and Mr Dove was to be manager.

3   Feebly Theo lay in bed and listened to his mother being rapturous about Dad moving up the ladder. Flabbily he sat on the sofa wrapped in a blanket while his bed was being carted off to the removal van. Totteringly he was helped into the car, and carried away into the sunset to the new flat.

4   He felt as if someone had slipped his backbone out, but he refused to go to bed.

5   "No way, Mum," he said. "Not on our first day here."

6   He sat in a chair near the kitchen door, with a smile forced on his face to match the one that flitted like sunshine across his mother's, as she cooked their first dinner. She kept interrupting the process every three minutes by running to the window and blissfully crying: "I can see the river. Oh, Ted, I can see the lovely hills. I've always wanted hills. And the smell of everything in here, Ted—all new and clean and painty!"

7   Ted was Mr Dove. Naturally there were plenty of things about his father that set Theo's teeth on edge. There was the way he held a fork, like a pencil, and the back of his neck, wrinkled exactly like a second forehead. Theo hated himself for finding anything at all about his father that he didn't like. But he was honest, and he had to admit these things.

8   But now, seeing his parents so happy, he was happy too. Whether that were the reason, or the new home was, or whatever, he began to feel steadily better.

9   It was great to wake up in the morning and not wish he was still asleep. Still, a week or so passed before he was fit enough to go downstairs and look around the place.

10   The flat was on the fifth floor of a ten-storey building. Theo walked slowly down the stairs, legs rickety, an odd sensation in his stomach. However, he reached the bottom and surveyed what was going to be the garden—a wasteland of raw soil, with a circle of trembling infant willows sticking up out of it, and a funny-shaped area of round river stones arranged around two bushes of dry sabre leaves edged in yellow. There was a fan of concrete which spread under the building to become the parking yard.

11   Theo shivered as he stepped outside, not because everything looked so stark, for time would fix that, but because the wind was like a knife. It smelled of burning leaves and a sweetish dampness, and he remembered that he had been indoors more than a month, the year had moved on, and very soon it would be winter. But he couldn't help liking everything, the serene clouds gliding over the huge sky, the smell of the river, the fact that he wouldn't have to change schools, but would continue to travel to Parramatta every day.

12   He felt that he'd be fine to walk up the stairs again, but he had promised his mother he'd go up in the lift. So he stepped into it. It, too, smelled of varnish, and new rubber flooring, and had golden lattice doors in an Oriental pattern, rather classy. He punched the button, and the lift moaned upwards.

13   It was then that Theo noticed he was not alone in the lift. There was something crouched in the back corner against the wall. For the first three seconds Theo thought it was some weird bundle of yuk that someone had left there. Then he saw it it pulsing slowly, like a sea anemone, and he realised it was alive.

14   He was stunned. There was no other word for it. He couldn't even move away from it, just stood there, freezing, staring. It was about the size of a medium dog, formless, as if it were made of three-quarters set jelly. It looked rather like jelly, too, with a faint sheen, almost like a slug. It was pearly grey, with darker, wet-looking areas.

15   The bottom of it spread out, as if it had melted a little, and near where its chest might have been were two half-formed blobs like hands or paws. It was rounded on top, as if for a head, but this bit was turned away towards the corner.

16   It gave off an unmistakable feeling of misery and helplessness. A long shudder passed over it, and two semi-circular bulges on the front of what Theo thought was its head began to quiver, like eyelids about to open.

17   Involuntarily Theo's mouth opened to let loose the kind of yell only heard in monster films, but all that came out was a croak. At that moment the lift stopped, the door wheezed open, and Theo stumbled out into the passage.

18   The world turned spangly black. Dimly he heard the lift moaning downwards, his mother speaking to him. He managed to walk, leaning on her, his eyes still shut because he was afraid to open them. He found himself on the living-room sofa, a cold wind blowing in from the balcony, a smell of cooking, everything normal. His mother clucked around.

19   "Too much for you. Shouldn't have let you go downstairs. Are you all right, darling? I wonder if I should call the doctor?"

20   Theo managed to say, "No, Mum. Silly. Okay now. Sorry," and sat up straight. It was true that his body was beginning to feel right, but his mind was going round and round, yelling desperately that he couldn't have seen that thing in the corner of the lift. He must have imagined it.

Adapted from a short story by Ruth Park

[END OF PASSAGE]

[BLANK PAGE]

FOR OFFICIAL USE

Total Mark

F

0860/402

NATIONAL QUALIFICATIONS 2010

THURSDAY, 29 APRIL 10.35 AM – 11.25 AM

ENGLISH STANDARD GRADE Foundation Level Reading Questions

Fill in these boxes and read what is printed below.

Full name of centre

Town

Forename

Surname

Date of birth

| Day | Month | Year | Scottish candidate number | Number of seat |

NB Before leaving the examination room you must give this booklet to the Invigilator. If you do not, you may lose all the marks for this paper.

Ma

QUESTIONS

Write your answers in the spaces provided.

Look at Paragraph 1.

1. Explain fully what happened to Theo around the time of his thirteenth birthday.

_____

_____   2   1

2. Write down **two** words from Paragraph 1 which show that he was fed up at this time.

[   ]   [   ]   2   1

3. " . . . not exactly ill, and not exactly well." (Paragraph 1)

Give **three** details from Paragraph 1 which show that Theo was "not exactly well".

(i) _____

(ii) _____

(iii) _____   2   1

Look at Paragraph 2.

4. Theo was affected by his illness.

(a) What sort of person was Theo before his illness?

_____

_____   2   1

(b) In what way did the illness change him?

_____   2

5. Why had the family moved house? Give **one** reason.

_____   2

PA
TO

Marks

Look at Paragraphs 3 to 7.

6. " . . . rapturous . . . " (Paragraph 3)

   Tick (✓) the box beside the best definition of "rapturous".

Suspicious	
Thrilled	
Angry	
Pleased	

   2 ■ 0

7. How was Theo's mother feeling "as she cooked their first dinner"? (Paragraph 6)

   Write down **one** piece of evidence from Paragraph 6 which shows this.

   Feeling: _____

   Evidence: _____   2 1 0

8. Explain fully why Theo "hated himself". (Paragraph 7)

   _____

   _____   2 ■ 0

Look at Paragraphs 8 to 11.

9. Theo "began to feel steadily better." (Paragraph 8)

   Give **two** possible reasons from Paragraph 8 why he began to feel better.

   (i) _____

   (ii) _____   2 1 0

10. What **three** things made Theo's journey down the stairs to the garden difficult?

    (i) _____

    (ii) _____

    (iii) _____   2 1 0

PAGE TOTAL

Mar

11. The garden downstairs was not very attractive.

(*a*) Write down **two** ways the writer shows us this in Paragraph 10.

_____   2 1

(*b*) Write down an expression from Paragraph 11 which shows that the garden will change.

_____   2 ■

12. " . . . the wind was like a knife." (Paragraph 11)

(*a*) What technique is the writer using in this expression? Tick (✓) the correct box.

Metaphor	
Rhyme	
Alliteration	
Simile	

2 ■

(*b*) What does this expression suggest about the wind?

_____   2 ■

13. What **two** things did Theo realise "as he stepped outside"? (Paragraph 11)

(i) _____

(ii) _____   2 1

Look at Paragraphs 12 to 15.

14. The lift in the building was new.

Write down **two** pieces of evidence which show that it was new.

(i) _____

(ii) _____   2 1

Marks

15. What made Theo realise that the thing in the lift was alive?

_____   2 ■ 0

16. "He was stunned." (Paragraph 14)

In what way has the writer made this sentence stand out?

_____   2 ■ 0

17. The creature in the lift was "like jelly" and "like a slug". (Paragraph 14)

Give **three** details which show this.

(i) _____

(ii) _____

(iii) _____   2 1 0

Look at Paragraphs 16 to 19.

18. Write down **two** words from Paragraph 16 which show that the creature was suffering.

    2 1 0

19. " . . . Theo stumbled out into the passage." (Paragraph 17)

What do you think happened to him next?

_____   2 ■ 0

20. "His mother clucked around." (Paragraph 18)

What does this suggest about the way Theo's mother behaved?

_____   2 ■ 0

[Turn over

PAGE TOTAL

Mar

Look at Paragraph 20.

21. "He must have imagined it." (Paragraph 20)

Why did Theo think he must have imagined the creature in the lift? Give **one** reason.

_____

2

Think about the passage as a whole.

22. What do you think will happen next in the story?

Tick (✓) **one** answer.

Theo will go back to the lift to investigate.	
Theo will try to forget the experience in the lift.	
Theo will tell his mum or dad and ask for help.	

Give **two** reasons from the passage which support your answer.

(i) _____

_____

(ii) _____

_____

2 **1**

[END OF QUESTION PAPER]

PAG
TOTA

FOR OFFICIAL USE

p2 ▢

p3 ▢

p4 ▢

p5 ▢

p6 ▢

TOTAL
MARK ▢

[BLANK PAGE]

[BLANK PAGE]

G

0860/403

NATIONAL QUALIFICATIONS 2010	THURSDAY, 29 APRIL 1.00 PM – 1.50 PM	ENGLISH STANDARD GRADE General Level Reading Text

Read carefully the passage overleaf. It will help if you read it twice. When you have done so, answer the questions. Use the spaces provided in the Question/Answer booklet.

CHIMPS GO APE IN ZOO

Ricky, Kindia, Quarzeh and all the rest—meet the chimpanzees who are now hanging out in Edinburgh's new plush £5·6 million property.

1 Ricky is munching slowly on the yellow of a hard-boiled egg, staring at the funny-looking fellow-primate on the other side of the glass. The 47-year-old chimpanzee once travelled the high seas on a merchant navy ship. Today he looks content, if slightly tired by the adventures of his youth. Crouching to introduce myself, I feel the urge to make small talk. "Hello Ricky . . . erm . . . enjoying your lunch?" He pauses, lifts an eyebrow in a recognisably snooty gesture, before turning to the more pressing business of scooping out the white of the egg from its cracked shell.

2 Ricky and the 10 other chimps at Edinburgh Zoo have every reason to feel a little superior. They have just moved into a state-of-the-art, air-conditioned, £5·6m luxury pad. Budongo Trail, which opens officially this weekend, is the largest chimpanzee enclosure in the world, and offers Ricky and his friends a higher standard of living than most humans will ever enjoy.

3 The complex is made up of three huge interconnected pods which open up into a gardened forest zone, complete with the longest, most intricate climbing frame ever built for apes. There's even a moat, which stops the water-shy chimps venturing too far, as well as adding to the sense of baronial splendour. Although the chimps are under observation, the place looks like too much fun to merit any comparison with the Big Brother house. It's more like a Crystal Maze set or the glamorous island hideaway of a James Bond baddie.

4 "They've moved from an ordinary house to a millionaire's mansion," beams Stephen Woollard, as he shows me round the place, justifiably proud of the structure he helped design. The education manager from the Royal Zoological Society of Scotland says the idea of a network that allowed scientists to study chimps in something like their natural environment was first proposed in the 1960s. He seems delighted this has finally been realised so spectacularly.

5 "Zoos have moved on from the old idea of looking at things lined up in cages, but we wanted to move it on further and set a whole new standard," he says. "It was something of a leap of faith, but the reaction has been tremendous. Everyone who sees the place says, 'Oh this is fantastic.'"

6 As we walk through the interactive exhibits, Woollard stops to explain how a cartoon game called Eddie Says, which lets children learn chimp gestures, was based on physical movements of none other than the zoologist himself. "Yes, they copied me, so I had to do all this sort of thing . . ." In an instant, Woollard becomes the perfect chimp, scrambling and hopping noisily around on the floor. "You see, it shouldn't be like a museum, where everything is hands-off. The kids will be running around, touching everything, as they should," he says.

7 Although the place appears to be one giant playground, the long glass frames of the enclosure pods also allow for serious study of animal behaviour. The project is linked to the conservation work of the Budongo Forest in north-west Uganda, where a team of researchers are gaining a better understanding of the threats faced by the forest's 600 or so chimpanzees. The population is falling because of habitat destruction and traps set for bush meat. The Royal Zoological Society of Scotland has been the primary sponsor of the African field station for the last three years, and many at Edinburgh Zoo have travelled there to gain further insight into chimp-life in the wild.

Characteristics of people

8 Laura McHugh is one of the lucky zoo-keeping researchers. The 23-year-old used her Ugandan adventure to learn how to differentiate between chimps. "It was amazing to see how the guys over there recognised each of the

chimps, knew their date of birth, and who was related to who," she enthuses. When McHugh came back to Scotland, it didn't take long to identify the zoo's residents. "You begin to recognise broad shoulders, say, or a slight beard. Now, to me, they have the characteristics of people."

9   The team at Budongo Trail cottoned on to the idea of giving the chimps celebrity status. There's Kindia, the boy-crazy teenager, and Lucy, the greedy guts of the gang. Visitors can even buy a glossy monthly magazine called Ape Vine!, packed full of the latest Budongo gossip. It's a good gimmick, but the personalities are far from manufactured. As we stare down into pod three, Quarzeh, the boisterous alpha male, is teaching nine-year-old Liberius how to tear up an egg carton. "It's too early to tell, but Liberius is potentially a future dominant male," McHugh explains. "He's still quite skinny though, so it's mostly just play-fights with his friend Kindia at the moment."

10   Ricky is also proving true to form as the loner with a shady past, eating lunch up on the glass window ledge, interacting with us rather than his hairy housemates. "Possibly because he was at sea, he does like being near humans," says McHugh. "But since coming to the Budongo Trail, he does engage in grooming a bit more." Professor Woollard concurs: "Yes,

he's had a bad start in life, and picked up some bad habits, but he's become more at ease."

Chimp culture

11   Staff say the apes are happier than ever before. The ceilings are four times as high as the zoo's previous enclosure, and even the soil is altered to copy the changing smells and textures of the wild. The sheer size of the place allows them freedom to separate in groups, spend time alone, or come together again to communicate.

12   "They do have the basics of language, and we're trying to discover what kind of level of language they have," Woollard explains. "It is possible there are many different dialects, since the dialect here in Edinburgh is different from chimps in Chester, or in Uganda. Do chimps have culture? We don't have all the answers." Chimp life reveals fresh marvels on a daily basis. Woollard believes visitors can help build a more complete behavioural picture by noting the quirks of the Budongo 11 as they go about their business. So, if you see Ricky when you visit Edinburgh Zoo, do say hello. The pleasantries might well have a purpose.

By Adam Forrest

[END OF PASSAGE]

[BLANK PAGE]

FOR OFFICIAL USE

G

Total Mark

0860/404

NATIONAL
QUALIFICATIONS
2010

THURSDAY, 29 APRIL
1.00 PM – 1.50 PM

ENGLISH
STANDARD GRADE
General Level
Reading
Questions

Fill in these boxes and read what is printed below.

Full name of centre

Town

Forename(s)

Surname

Date of birth

Day   Month   Year   Scottish candidate number   Number of seat

**NB Before leaving the examination room you must give this booklet to the Invigilator.
If you do not, you may lose all the marks for this paper.**

SA 0860/404 6/57710

Ma

QUESTIONS

Write your answers in the spaces provided.

Look at Paragraphs 1 and 2.

1. Where exactly is the writer at the start of the passage?

   _____   2 | 1

2. In Paragraph 1, the writer makes Ricky the chimp seem human.
   Give **two** examples from Paragraph 1 of Ricky's "human" behaviour.

   (i) _____

   (ii) _____   2 | 1

3. In Paragraph 1, the writer introduces himself to Ricky.
   Describe Ricky's reaction when the writer speaks to him.

   _____

   _____   2 | 1

4. Give **three** reasons why, according to the writer, the chimps have "every reason to feel a little superior". (Paragraph 2)

   (i) _____

   (ii) _____

   (iii) _____   2 | 1

Look at Paragraphs 3 to 5.

5. Explain how the design of the "forest zone" (Paragraph 3) helps the chimps keep **both** active **and** safe.

   _____

   _____   2 | 1

Marks

6. Write down **two** expressions from Paragraph 4 which show the contrast between the chimps' new enclosure and their old home.

2 ■ 0

7. Explain fully why the new enclosure is useful to scientists.

_____

_____

2 1 0

8. Stephen Woollard, the zoo's education manager, is both "proud" and "delighted" about the new enclosure. (Paragraph 4)

In your own words, explain why he is **both** "proud" **and** "delighted".

Proud _____

Delighted _____

2 1 0

Look at Paragraphs 6 and 7.

9. " . . . we walk through the interactive exhibits." (Paragraph 6)

Show how the idea of "interactive exhibits" is continued in this paragraph.

_____

_____

2 1 0

10. Which of the following expressions best sums up Stephen Woollard's attitude to the interactive exhibits? Tick (✓) **one** box.

Rather uninterested	
Very enthusiastic	
Slightly critical	

Give a reason from the passage to support your answer.

_____

2 1 0

Ma

11. What evidence is there that the enclosure is part of a serious, international "study of animal behaviour"? (Paragraph 7)

_____

_____   2 1

12. **In your own words**, explain why the chimp population in Uganda is falling.

_____

_____   2 1

Look at Paragraphs 8 to 10.

13. ". . . differentiate between chimps." (Paragraph 8)

Tick (✓) the box beside the meaning of "differentiate between".

To study closely	
To help	
To relate to	
To tell apart	

2

14. The chimps have been given "celebrity status". (Paragraph 9)

(*a*) In what **two** ways are the chimps like human celebrities?

_____

_____   2 1

(*b*) Why do you think the team decided to give the chimps "celebrity status"?

_____

_____   2

Marks

15. ". . . greedy guts of the gang."

". . . good gimmick." (Paragraph 9)

Identify the technique used in these expressions.

_____   2 ■ 0

16. **In your own words**, explain what we learn about Liberius' place in the chimp group.

_____

_____   2 1 0

17. Ricky's "bad start in life" had led to "some bad habits". (Paragraph 10)

(a) Give **one** example of Ricky's "bad habits".

_____   2 ■ 0

(b) How do we know that he is now "more at ease" with the other chimps?

_____   2 ■ 0

Look at Paragraphs 11 and 12.

18. ". . . the apes are happier than ever before." (Paragraph 11)

Give **three** reasons for this.

(i) _____

(ii) _____

(iii) _____   2 1 0

19. In Paragraph 12, Professor Woollard discusses the language of the chimps.

In your own words, explain what he means by "different dialects".

_____

_____   2 1 0

[Turn over

PAGE
TOTAL

Mar

20. "Chimp life reveals fresh marvels on a daily basis." (Paragraph 12)

Explain **in your own words** what the writer means by this.

_____

_____   2 1

21. How can visitors to the zoo help the scientists?

_____

_____   2 1

Think about the passage as a whole.

22. "CHIMPS GO APE IN ZOO"

Give **two** reasons why this is a suitable headline for this article.

(i) _____

(ii) _____   2 1

23. What is the main purpose of this passage? Tick (✓) the best answer.

To argue that animals like chimps should not be kept in zoos.	
To give a positive, informative view of the new enclosure.	
To request donations for the upkeep of the new enclosure.	

Give **one** piece of evidence from the passage to support your answer.

_____   2 1

[END OF QUESTION PAPER]

PAG
TOT

FOR OFFICIAL USE

p2 ☐

p3 ☐

p4 ☐

p5 ☐

p6 ☐

TOTAL
MARK ☐

FOR OFFICIAL USE

[BLANK PAGE]

[BLANK PAGE]

F

0860/401

NATIONAL
QUALIFICATIONS
2011

FRIDAY, 6 MAY
10.35 AM – 11.25 AM

ENGLISH
STANDARD GRADE
Foundation Level
Reading
Text

Read carefully the passage overleaf. It will help if you read it twice. When you have done so, answer the questions. Use the spaces provided in the Question/Answer booklet.

In this extract from a novel, a young girl named Lucy has a strange experience.

1   School was over and the Easter holidays had begun. Lucy was walking home, between the reed banks, along the marsh road, when it started to happen. She had just come to the small bridge, where the road goes over the deep water. She called this Otterfeast Bridge, because once she had seen an otter on the edge of it, over the black water, eating an eel. That had been three years before. But she still felt excitement whenever she came to this part of the road, and she always looked ahead eagerly, towards the bridge.

2   Today, as usual, the bridge was empty. As she crossed over it, she looked between the rails, into the black water. She always did this, just in case there might be an otter down there, in the water, looking up at her, or maybe swimming beneath at that very moment.

3   And today, there was something. But what was it, down there in the water? She leaned over the rail and peered.

4   Something deep in the dark water, something white, kept twisting. A fish?

5   Suddenly she knew. It was an eel—behaving in the strangest way. At first, she thought it must be two eels, fighting. But no, it was just one eel. It knotted itself and unknotted. Then it swam quickly round in circles, corkscrewing over and over as it went. At one point, its tail flipped right out of the water. Then it was writhing down into the mud, setting a grey cloud drifting. Then it was up at the surface again, bobbing its head into the air. She saw its beaky face, then its little mouth opening. She saw the pale inside of its mouth.

6   Then it was writhing and tumbling in a knot. Quite a small eel, only a foot long.

7   As it danced its squirming, circling, darting dance, it was drifting along in the current of the water. Soon she lost sight of it under the water shine. Then, twenty yards downstream, she saw its head bob up again. Then a swirl and it vanished. Then up again, bob, bob, bob.

8   What was wrong with it? Seeing its peculiar head bobbing up like that, and its little mouth opening, she had felt a painful twist somewhere in her middle. She had wanted to scoop the eel up and help it. It needed help. Something was wrong with it.

9   At that moment, staring along the dimpled shine of the water where it curved away among the tall reeds, she felt something else.

10   At first, she had no idea what made her head go dizzy and her feet stagger. She gripped the bridge rail and braced her feet apart. She thought she had felt the rail itself give her hand a jolt.

11   What was it?

12   "Garronk! Garronk! Garraaaaaark!"

13   The floppy, untidy shape of a heron was scrambling straight up out of the reed beds. It did not flap away in stately slow motion, like an ordinary heron. It flailed and hoisted itself up, exactly as if it were bounding up an invisible spiral stair. Then, from a great height, it tumbled away towards the sea beyond the marsh. Something had scared it badly. But what? Something in the marsh had frightened it. And seeing the heron so frightened frightened Lucy.

14   The marsh was always a lonely place. Now she felt the loneliness. As she stood there, looking up, the whole bluish and pinky sky of soft cloud moved slowly. She looked again along the water, where the reeds leaned all one way, bowing gently in the light wind. The eel was no longer to be seen. Was it still writhing and bobbing its head up, as the slow flow carried it away through the marsh? She looked down into the water, under the bridge. The black water moved silently, crumpling and twirling little whorls of light.

15   Then it came again. Beneath her feet the bridge road jumped and the rail jarred her hand. At the same moment, the surface of the water was blurred by a sudden mesh of tiny ripples all over it.

16   An earthquake! It must be an earthquake.

17   A completely new kind of fear gripped Lucy. For a few seconds she did not dare to move. The thought of the bridge collapsing and dropping her into the water with its writhing eels was bad enough. But the thought of the marsh itself opening a great crack, and herself and all the water and mud and eels and reeds pouring into bottomless black, maybe right into the middle of the earth, was worse. She felt her toes curling like claws and the soles of her feet prickling with electricity.

18   Quickly then she began to walk—but it was like walking on a bouncy narrow plank between skyscrapers. She lifted each foot carefully and set it down firmly and yet gently. As fast as she dared, and yet quite slow. But soon—she couldn't help it—she started running. What if that earthquake shock had brought the ceiling down on her mother? Or even shaken the village flat, like dominoes? And what if some great towering piece of machinery, at the factory, had toppled on to her father?

19   And then, as she ran, it came again, pitching her off balance, so that her left foot hit her right calf and down she went. As she lay there, flat and winded, it came again. This time, the road seemed to hit her chest and stomach, a strong, hard thump. Then another. And each time, she saw the road gravel under her face jump slightly. And it was then, as she lay there, that she heard the weirdest sound. Nothing like any bird she had ever heard. It came from out of the marsh behind her. It was a long wailing cry, like a fire-engine siren. She jumped up and began to run blindly.

From "The Iron Woman" by Ted Hughes

[END OF PASSAGE]

[BLANK PAGE]

FOR OFFICIAL USE

F

Total
Mark

0860/402

NATIONAL
QUALIFICATIONS
2011

FRIDAY, 6 MAY
10.35 AM – 11.25 AM

ENGLISH
STANDARD GRADE
Foundation Level
Reading
Questions

Fill in these boxes and read what is printed below.

Full name of centre

Town

Forename(s)

Surname

Date of birth

Day   Month   Year   Scottish candidate number   Number of seat

**NB Before leaving the examination room you must give this booklet to the Invigilator.
If you do not, you may lose all the marks for this paper.**

Ma

QUESTIONS

Write your answers in the spaces provided.

Look at Paragraph 1.

1. **Where** and **when** does the story begin?

    Where _____

    When _____   2 1

2. Why did Lucy call the bridge "Otterfeast Bridge"?

    _____

    _____   2 1

3. Write down **two** words from Paragraph 1 which show that Lucy found "this part of the road" thrilling.

    [   ]   [   ]   2 1

Look at Paragraphs 3 and 4.

4. Write down **two** ways the writer suggests that Lucy was uncertain about what she saw.

    (i) _____

    (ii) _____   2 1

Look at Paragraph 5.

5. The eel was "behaving in the strangest way." (Paragraph 5)

    Write down **two** things it did which were strange.

    (i) _____

    (ii) _____   2 1

PAG
TOT

Marks

Look at Paragraphs 6 to 8.

6. "Quite a small eel." (Paragraph 6)

   Why might Lucy be surprised by this?

   _____

   _____   2 ■ 0

7. ". . . its squirming, circling, darting dance . . ." (Paragraph 7)

   Explain fully what these words suggest about **how** the eel was moving.

   _____

   _____   2 1 0

8. ". . . bob, bob, bob." (Paragraph 7)

   Why does the writer repeat the word "bob"?

   _____   2 1 0

9. As Lucy watched the eel,

   (*a*) how did she feel?

   _____   2 ■ 0

   (*b*) what did she want to do?

   _____   2 ■ 0

Look at Paragraphs 10 to 14.

10. When the bridge shook, what **two** things did Lucy do to keep herself steady?

    (i) _____

    (ii) _____   2 1 0

[Turn over

PAGE
TOTAL

Ma~

11. "What was it?" (Paragraph 11)

In what way does the writer make this sentence stand out?

_____   2

12. "Garronk! Garronk! Garraaaaaak!" (Paragraph 12)

Why does the writer use these words?

_____

_____   2   1

13. The heron was "scrambling . . . out of the reed beds." (Paragraph 13)

Write down another word from this paragraph which shows that the heron moved clumsily.

2

14. "Now she felt the loneliness." (Paragraph 14)

Why did Lucy feel like this?

_____   2

15. Lucy looked around as she stood on the bridge.

Write down **three** things she could see.

(i) _____

(ii) _____

(iii) _____   2   1

PAG
TOT~

Marks

Look at Paragraphs 15 to 17.

16. Explain fully why Lucy thought it was an earthquake.

_____

_____   2 | 1 | 0

17. What do you think the writer means by "a completely new kind of fear"?

_____   2 | ■ | 0

18. ". . . bottomless black . . ." (Paragraph 17)

    What technique is the writer using in this expression? Tick (✓) the correct box.

Metaphor	
Simile	
Rhyme	
Alliteration	

2 | ■ | 0

Look at Paragraph 18 to the end of the passage.

19. When Lucy began to walk, why did it feel "like walking on a bouncy narrow plank between skyscrapers"? (Paragraph 18)

_____

_____   2 | 1 | 0

20. Explain fully what Lucy was worrying about as she ran away.

_____

_____   2 | 1 | 0

[Turn over

PAGE
TOTAL

Ma

21. Why did the gravel under Lucy's face "jump slightly"? (Paragraph 19)

_____   2 1

22. Lucy heard "the weirdest sound." (Paragraph 19)

How does the writer show that the sound was weird?

_____   2

Think about the passage as a whole.

23. Write down **one** piece of evidence from the passage which shows Lucy is an **imaginative** girl.

_____   2

24. What do you think Lucy will do next? Tick (✓) **one** answer.

Lucy will rush back home to her parents.	
Lucy will run away and get lost in the marsh.	

Give **two** pieces of evidence from the passage to support your answer.

(i) _____

(ii) _____   2 1

[END OF QUESTION PAPER]

FOR OFFICIAL USE

p2	
p3	
p4	
p5	
p6	
TOTAL MARK	

[BLANK PAGE]

STANDARD GRADE | GENERAL

2011
READING

[BLANK PAGE]

G

0860/403

NATIONAL
QUALIFICATIONS
2011

FRIDAY, 6 MAY
1.00 PM – 1.50 PM

ENGLISH
STANDARD GRADE
General Level
Reading
Text

Read carefully the passage overleaf. It will help if you read it twice. When you have done so, answer the questions. Use the spaces provided in the Question/Answer booklet.

In this passage the writer describes a childhood visit to Glasgow at Christmas.

BRIGHT LIGHTS BIG CITY

1   Glasgow didn't have Christmas, it *was* Christmas. Even I knew that. A small-town seasider who would never swim, a child thrilled by beauty who somehow managed to break every glass ornament she ever touched, I knew the difference between magic and cold reality. Our town had miles of seaweed and pink rock with writing through it, cows and rolling greenery. We had industrial-strength downpours of rain. Glasgow people came to us in the summer holidays, desperate for sunburn, seagulls and seafood. But sea breezes and face-filing sand counted for nothing in winter. Nothing desirable, at least. At the opposite end of the year, as the dark descended, people wanted the city; for dazzle, the warmth of crowds and snowy shop displays. The place for cheer, therefore, was at the other end of the train line. Glasgow. My sister worked there in a stockbroker's office, typing important letters she did not understand, and claimed the city was what counted. "Our town is a dump," she'd say, rolling her eyes. "We've only a daft wee tree at the War Memorial. Glasgow's got hundreds. Lights and everything, George Square, you canny imagine it. Glasgow's the works!"

2   I got to see what those works were for the first time in December, 1961. I was five, and for the occasion dressed in a red Peter Pan collar coat and white nylon gloves.

3   "You've got to look nice for Santa," my mother said, scouring the side of my mouth with a spit-doused hankie till it hurt. "He lives up the stairs in the store," she explained, checking my face for further signs of imperfection, laziness and disease. The journey, it seemed, was putting us on show. "You keep they gloves on and mind they're new. One mark and you're for it, lady."

4   Whatever "it" was, I knew to steer clear.

5   The train was cold and the seats kitted out in dark, shiny tartan. An overhead rack hung like a hammock on a wooden frame, waiting for luggage. "Touch nothing," my mother said. "The windows are filthy." There was no arguing. Our view was strips of grass and passing branches, visible in glimpses through grime. Central Station, however, supplied the journey's missing sense of space. It was big enough for trains to roll right inside and from my vantage point, some three feet from the ground, high as cliffs. The noise of our footsteps over the platform shook waves into puddles as we passed. A bouquet of pigeons with rose-pink chests opened like roses. That was the size of the place: there were pigeons indoors, a clock the size of our bathroom. I tripped over my own feet, staring.

6   Outside, Glasgow presented itself: a black city. The buildings were coated with velvet-deep soot. There were charcoal-coloured statues at office doors or holding up second and third storeys of buildings. My mother hauled me by the hand down a long corridor of ash-grey walls and matching sky, my face brushing against the tweedy coats of strangers, to—my mother's words—the fanciest shop in the world. There was a Christmas tree inside the door, a sour reek of adult perfume. The grotto, three floors up, was a room full of glittery cotton wool and animal cut-outs, with a red-suited man in a squinty beard, the elastic of which stretched too far beneath his ears. I would not sit on his knee and my mother was embarrassed. When I resisted two shoves, she lifted me by the arms and sat me there, whether he or I liked it or not. Santa looked tired, and I felt uncomfortable. My failure to respond when asked what I wanted for Christmas did not throw him. It must have happened several times that day. He gave me my gift and released me back to the wild. The gift itself was a pink manicure set with sequins on the front. It had scissors and little metal sticks that looked like miniature butcher's tools. Whatever they were for, it was lovely. It took a moment to work out this was mine to keep. I did not need to hand it back for another little girl. The little pink cutlery set was mine.

7   We shared a vanilla ice cream in the store's café then stood on the stairs to see their display of lights and bells from above. "We're like angels," my mother said, her mouth pale now she'd eaten her lipstick off on a scone.

8   The food apart, nothing was bought. Odd though it seems now, in an age where people take day trips to shopping centres for pleasure, we had not come for the shopping. We had come for the promised lights, which we could not, according to my sister, imagine for ourselves. She was right. I remember still the eye-watering colour strung between high buildings, the never-ending sky with no stars. But the bit that took my breath away was entirely natural. It was starlings: thousands upon thousands of starlings in George Square, a chorus of birds clinging or swooping between telegraph wires, the reckless, nerve-shredding noise of screaming.

9   My mother had to pull me away to get the train. All the way back, I knew my sister was right. I would not have imagined any of it. But what was magic, what stayed with me and always would, was not the lights or the trees, not the manicure set from a man who was not Santa at all.

10   It was the birds. Little creatures making what life they could in the city square, singing for dear life and thriving. I'd never have imagined the courage, the grandeur of those birds. I got told off on the way home for making my gloves black, of course. I'd not get to go again. But it was worth it. In one visit and forever, the noise of a real chorus that has never lost its volume, its truth.

11   The starlings have long gone from George Square. No matter. First thing on Christmas morning, we go out feeding birds. It seems the right thing to do.

Adapted from a newspaper article by Janice Galloway

[END OF PASSAGE]

[BLANK PAGE]

FOR OFFICIAL USE

G

Total Mark

0860/404

NATIONAL
QUALIFICATIONS
2011

FRIDAY, 6 MAY
1.00 PM – 1.50 PM

ENGLISH
STANDARD GRADE
General Level
Reading
Questions

Fill in these boxes and read what is printed below.

Full name of centre

Town

Forename(s)

Surname

Date of birth

Day   Month   Year   Scottish candidate number   Number of seat

NB Before leaving the examination room you must give this booklet to the Invigilator. If you do not, you may lose all the marks for this paper.

Ma

QUESTIONS

Write your answers in the spaces provided.

Look at Paragraph 1.

1. "Glasgow didn't have Christmas, it *was* Christmas." (Paragraph 1)

    What do you think the writer means by this?

    _____   2

2. Explain **one** of the two surprising things the writer tells us about herself.

    _____

    _____   2   1

3. ". . . sunburn, seagulls and seafood." (Paragraph 1)

    Identify the technique used here.

    _____   2

4. Glasgow was more popular than the seaside in the winter. Give **three** things Glasgow could offer in winter that the writer's town could not.

    (i)   _____

    (ii) _____

    (iii) _____   2   1

5. Write down **one** thing the writer's sister **did** and **one** thing she **said** which showed her view of her town.

    _____

    _____   2   1

PAG
TOT

Marks

Look at Paragraphs 2 to 4.

6. Give **two** details which show that preparing to travel to Glasgow was not pleasant for the writer.

_____

_____ | 2 | 1 | 0 |

7. "Whatever "it" was, I knew to steer clear." (Paragraph 4)

    In what way does the writer make this statement stand out?

_____ | 2 | ■ | 0 |

Look at Paragraph 5.

8. **In your own words**, explain what spoiled the view out of the train window on the way to Glasgow.

_____

_____ | 2 | 1 | 0 |

9. "Central Station, however, supplied the journey's missing sense of space." (Paragraph 5)

    Give **two** ways in which the writer shows the "space" of Central Station.

_____

_____ | 2 | 1 | 0 |

10. "A bouquet of pigeons with rose-pink chests opened like roses." (Paragraph 5)

    (*a*) Identify **two** techniques used here.

    _____ | 2 | 1 | 0 |

    (*b*) Explain what the pigeons are doing.

    _____ | 2 | ■ | 0 |

[Turn over

Ma

Look at Paragraph 6.

11. ". . . a black city." (Paragraph 6)

How does the writer continue this idea in Paragraph 6?

_____

_____   2   1

12. Give **one** piece of evidence which shows that the streets were crowded.

_____   2   ■

13. Explain the use of the dashes in the expression "–my mother's words–". (Paragraph 6)

_____

_____   2   1

14. **In your own words**, explain why the Santa costume was not convincing.

_____

_____   2   1

15. What did the writer's mother do to make her sit on "Santa's" knee?

_____

_____   2   1

16. Write down **two** expressions which show the writer's confusion about what the gift was.

_____

_____   2   1

Marks

17. **In your own words**, explain fully how the writer felt about receiving the gift.

_____

_____ 2 1 0

Look at Paragraphs 7 and 8.

18. In what way were the writer and her mother "like angels"?

_____ 2 ■ 0

19. What was "odd" about the shopping trip?

_____ 2 ■ 0

20. Explain fully why the starlings made such an impression on the writer when she first saw them.

_____

_____ 2 1 0

Read Paragraph 9 to the end of the passage.

21. Give **two** pieces of evidence from Paragraph 9 which show the writer really enjoyed this outing.

_____

_____ 2 1 0

22. "But it was worth it." (Paragraph 10)

Why was the writer in trouble on the way home and why was it "worth it"?

_____

_____ 2 1 0

[Turn over

PAGE
TOTAL

Ma

23. The visit made a lasting impression on the writer. In what way does she show this in Paragraph 11?

_____

2   1

Think about the passage as a whole.

24. Do you think the writer gives a realistic description of this childhood experience? Give **one** piece of evidence from the passage to support your answer.

Yes	
No	

_____

_____

2

[END OF QUESTION PAPER]

PAG
TOT

FOR OFFICIAL USE

p2	
p3	
p4	
p5	
p6	
TOTAL MARK	

[BLANK PAGE]

[BLANK PAGE]

F

0860/27/11

NATIONAL   THURSDAY, 26 APRIL   ENGLISH
QUALIFICATIONS   10.35 AM – 11.25 AM   STANDARD GRADE
2012   Foundation Level
                                               Reading
                                               Text

Read carefully the passage overleaf. It will help if you read it twice. When you have done so, answer the questions. Use the spaces provided in the Question/Answer booklet.

In this article, the writer describes her experiences catching snakes in Swaziland.

1   **IT'S PAST MIDNIGHT** when the telephone rings. I drag myself out of bed.

2   The woman on the other end of the phone is hysterical. Her name is Sanele, and she is crying and screaming. Between her sobs, I can hear a young child in the background shouting, "It's coming in: the snake is coming in!" From Sanele's frenzied description, I manage to establish that a large, slender snake has reached the doorway, trapping her toddler and baby daughter. It is about 3m long—probably a black mamba, I think to myself (mamba is a Zulu word meaning "big snake"). Still in pyjamas, I grab my trusty snake tongs—a gadget for handling snakes that resembles a park keeper's litter-grabber—and rush off into the rainy night.

3   As I drive to the farm, I feel more certain of the mystery snake's identity. Black mambas are highly inquisitive and frequently enter people's homes, seeking refuge in schoolbags and cupboards and under beds—anywhere they can squeeze into. Like many other reptiles, they look for a cool location when the summer heat becomes unbearable, and a nice warm spot during the winter. Unfortunately, houses fit the bill perfectly.

4   The rain is coming down in bucketloads now. I try to keep my vehicle on the muddy track through the sugarcane fields, steering with one hand and holding my mobile phone to my ear with the other. Sanele begs me to hurry, blurting that her one and only candle has almost burned out. Tears of relief stream down my own face when, after an hour, I find the farm at last.

DICING WITH DEATH

5   Sanele is standing perilously close to the curled up mamba, holding her broom like a weapon, ready to bash the intruder to a pulp if it dares move another inch. This is a fatal mistake—no mamba I have ever come across will just wait by while you take a hefty swing at it. Instead, it will strike with deadly accuracy. Rule number 1: if you are close enough to kill a snake, it is most certainly close enough to kill you.

6   Using my tongs, I carefully remove the creature and pop it in a snake bag. Sanele immediately rushes forwards to hug her children, and I complete the rescue by teaching the correct first-aid procedure and explaining the basics of snake safety. As usual, I emphasise the importance of staying still when in close proximity to a venomous snake.

7   There's a very good reason for this: snakes sense what's going on around them in a completely different way to us. Since snakes have poor eyesight, sudden, jerky movements that take them by surprise are almost guaranteed to upset them. So if you ever find yourself face to face with a black mamba, it is essential to keep calm. The snake will strike defensively only if it senses threatening movement.

KEEP YOUR DISTANCE

8   Mambas belong to the family which also contains the cobras and sea snakes—species equally feared for their powerful venom. One of four species of mamba, the black is named not for the colour of its body—it is brownish, olive or greyish overall—but for the inky black lining to its mouth. If cornered, it flicks its jaws open to reveal this bold colour as a warning to keep your distance. To make sure its threat is understood, the snake lifts its head well off the ground, flattens its neck into a slight hood and gives a hollow-sounding hiss. It's an altogether frightening display.

9   The black mamba has a reputation for being extremely aggressive. It is said to be able to outrun a person on a horse and to 'stare' at its victims as if to spook them. Some local people even believe that black mambas hunt humans. All of these claims are totally wrong. In my experience, black mambas will more often than not do their best to get away as quickly as possible, slithering towards the nearest hollow tree, termite mound, burrow or dark corner. They become aggressive only when there is no escape route.

10   In the meantime, the snake-rescuer's life is a busy one. Every season I rescue about 600 snakes, of which 100 or so are black mambas. I run *Antivenom Swazi*, a charity whose

mission is to raise enough funds to create a 'bank' of anti-venom for treating snakebite victims in Swaziland, a small country beside South Africa. My plan is to store the anti-venom in two different locations, so that everyone can get some within two hours.

11   Speed is essential. Mamba venom is fast-acting. The bite itself is usually not very painful with little or no swelling, but the first symptoms are felt within 15 minutes—much sooner if the victim is a small child. Breathing difficulties develop rapidly, leading to death within a few hours. Just two drops of venom are fatal, and a mamba may deliver as much as 10 times that amount in a single bite; each individual mamba has enough venom to kill up to 14 adult humans.

12   Snakebite in Africa is becoming much more common. Farmers in Swaziland are particularly at risk, because farms are ideal mamba habitat. The dense fields of sugarcane and maize are full of prey: rats, mice, gerbils, shrews, small birds and sometimes baby chicks are all taken. The mambas come out just after sunrise, climbing up the cane or maize to about chest height, then stay in the sun for an hour or two before moving away to hunt. In the late afternoon, they slink off to their lairs for the night.

13   Anti-venom—the only cure—is not easily available in Swaziland, and in any case is so expensive that locals can't afford it. Eighty per cent of the country's population rely on traditional healers, who prescribe a herbal medicine known as *mooty* to treat snakebite. But while such remedies can be effective for some illnesses, they are useless against the powerful venom of a mamba.

IN THE NICK OF TIME

14   The phone rings again. It is the second time that I have received a call for help from this particular farm, which is situated in dense bush. It is a long drive on a bad dirt road. When I finally arrive, I am met by a frantic father and his family, who physically drag me out of my vehicle. I am rushed into the house, where I find a young boy lying in bed. On top of the sheet is a huge mamba.

15   We freeze. If we make a mistake or the child moves, there's a very good chance he will be bitten. I try to calm him and edge towards the snake and lift it off the child in one smooth motion. Luckily, the previous snake-safety course I gave at this farm has saved the youngster from a fatal bite.

16   It's a happy ending this time. Black mambas are part of our lives, whether we like it or not, and we must learn to live with them.

Adapted from an article in
BBC Wildlife Magazine

[END OF PASSAGE]

[BLANK PAGE]

FOR OFFICIAL USE

Total Mark

F

0860/27/01

NATIONAL
QUALIFICATIONS
2012

THURSDAY, 26 APRIL
10.35 AM – 11.25 AM

ENGLISH
STANDARD GRADE
Foundation Level
Reading
Questions

Fill in these boxes and read what is printed below.

Full name of centre

Town

Forename(s)

Surname

Date of birth

Day   Month   Year   Scottish candidate number   Number of seat

NB Before leaving the examination room you must give this booklet to the Invigilator. If you do not, you may lose all the marks for this paper.

Mar

QUESTIONS

Write your answers in the spaces provided.

Look at Paragraphs 1 and 2.

1. Give a reason from Paragraph 1 why the telephone call might be inconvenient for the writer.

    _____ 2

2. "The woman on the other end of the phone is hysterical." (Paragraph 2)

    Write down two other words from Paragraph 2 which continue this idea.

    2　1

3. Give **two** pieces of evidence that the writer left in a hurry to help the woman.

    _____

    _____ 2　1

Look at Paragraphs 3 and 4.

4. Name **three** places where snakes hide in houses.

    (i) _____

    (ii) _____

    (iii) _____ 2　1

5. Explain fully why houses "fit the bill perfectly" as shelters for snakes. (Paragraph 3)

    _____

    _____ 2　1

Marks

6. Give **two** reasons why the writer finds it difficult to drive in Paragraph 4.

_____

_____   2 | 1 | 0

Look at Paragraphs 5, 6 and 7.

7. **Write down** an expression from Paragraph 5 which shows that Sanele is in great danger when the writer arrives.

_____   2 | ■ | 0

8. Give **two** pieces of advice from the writer about what to do if you see a snake.

_____

_____   2 | 1 | 0

9. What can snakes **not** do very well?

_____   2 | ■ | 0

10. What is the **only** reason why a snake might attack a human?

_____

_____   2 | ■ | 0

Look at Paragraphs 8 and 9.

11. What is surprising about the name "black mamba"? (Paragraph 8)

_____   2 | ■ | 0

12. If a mamba is cornered, what is the first thing it does **and** why does it do this?

_____

_____   2 | 1 | 0

[Turn over

Ma

13. Name **three** other things a mamba does when it is cornered.

(i) _____

(ii) _____

(iii) _____   2 1

14. Read the following statements. Tick (✓) the correct box to show whether each statement is TRUE, FALSE or CANNOT TELL from the Passage.

	True	False	Cannot Tell
Black mambas try to escape quickly if disturbed.			
Black mambas stare at prey to hypnotise them.			
Black mambas are aggressive if defending young.			
Black mambas are faster than people on horses.			

2

2

2

2

Look at Paragraphs 10 and 11.

15. Explain fully what *Antivenom Swazi* will do with the money it raises.

_____

_____   2 1

16. Why, at first, might someone bitten by a mamba **not** think it was serious?
Give **two** reasons.

_____

_____   2 1

17. Write down **two** separate expressions showing that mamba venom is fast-acting or deadly.

_____

_____   2 1

Marks

Look at Paragraphs 12 and 13.

18. Give **one** reason why farms ". . . are ideal mamba habitat." (Paragraph 12)

_____

2 ■ 0

19. Explain fully why 80% of people in Swaziland "rely on traditional healers" instead of using anti-venom.

_____

_____

2 1 0

Look at Paragraph 14 to the end of the passage.

20. In Paragraph 14, the writer receives another call for help.

   Write down two words which show that the family is panicking when she arrives.

2 1 0

21. "We freeze." (Paragraph 15)

   Give **one** way the writer has made this sentence stand out.

_____

2 ■ 0

[Turn over

PAGE
TOTAL

Ma

Think about the passage as a whole.

22. What is the message of this passage? Tick (✓) **one** box.

Snakes are dangerous and should be killed.	
Snakes can be dangerous and should be treated carefully.	
Snakes are not dangerous and can be tamed.	

Give **one** piece of evidence from the passage to support your choice.

_____   2   1

[END OF QUESTION PAPER]

PA
TO

FOR OFFICIAL USE

p2	
p3	
p4	
p5	
p6	
TOTAL MARK	

[BLANK PAGE]

STANDARD GRADE | GENERAL

2012
READING

[BLANK PAGE]

G

0860/29/11

NATIONAL
QUALIFICATIONS
2012

THURSDAY, 26 APRIL
1.00 PM – 1.50 PM

ENGLISH
STANDARD GRADE
General Level
Reading
Text

Read carefully the passage overleaf. It will help if you read it twice. When you have done so, answer the questions. Use the spaces provided in the Question/Answer booklet.

THREE MEN AND A DOG

You don't need to lug a tent on a long-distance walk in the Lakes. Kevin Rushby and his two sons discover barn camping on a rite of passage hike with their young hound.

1 It's so easy when they're puppies. You stroll down the street and they come home exhausted. People stop and have conversations.

2 "Aren't you gorgeous?" (That can be disappointing, of course: it's the dog who is being addressed, not you). Then they get bigger. They want proper walks. They want sticks thrown. We got a mongrel terrier pup from a rescue centre. And when Wilf reached full size, I started looking to take him for a decent walk in deep countryside—a rite of passage for a young hound, somewhere beyond the realm of the dreaded poo bin. There were two teenage sons too, Con and Niall, and they seemed surprisingly enthusiastic—there's one tip for getting your kids to walk: buy or borrow a dog.

3 The Lake District seemed a good choice—plenty of wonderful walking there—but with snow on the way I didn't fancy camping. Instead, I booked us into a couple of barns. There's a whole slew of them across the Lakes, offering varying degrees of comfort from downright basic to . . . well, let's call it cosily austere. Nevertheless, they did seem to offer a cushier alternative to tents.

4 Our hotel in Keswick was willing to take a dog for a night in one of their dog-friendly rooms, so we planned on a comfortable start followed by three days of walking in a great horseshoe around the southern extremities of Borrowdale.

5 I have this fond vision of dogs in hotels and pubs. It's an affable labrador-type creature laid out under the table, snoozing. At the hotel, Wilf isn't like that. He runs riot. He loves hotels. He loves the way people drop crisps in the bar. He sneaks into a neighbour's room and sniffs their luggage for food. Curiously, they laugh indulgently and say things like, "You're a lovable chap, aren't you?" A dog's life doesn't seem so bad, really. Wilf soon settles down on his dedicated luxury bed and sleeps like a baby. I spend the night half-awake, stirring at every doggy snort, worrying that he'll get up and cock his leg on the four-poster. Mercifully that doesn't happen.

6 At first light, we set out. Winter walking means every hour of daylight is precious. We soon leave Keswick behind and climb steadily on to the ridge of High Seat. The weather forecast is for snow showers, but all we get is mist and cloud and occasional tantalising glimpses of Derwent Water below. On Bleaberry Fell, Wilf disappears for 10 minutes and I fear he will return with one of the black grouse that are chuckling at us from afar (not a sheep, we took the precaution of stock-training him before the trip, and anyway he would look silly as he's only knee-height to a ewe). He eventually reappears, grouseless, bounding across clumps of heather as if he's on springs.

7 We eat our lunch looking down at Watendlath, perhaps the most idyllic of Lakeland settings. Then we march down to Rosthwaite in Borrowdale and search out our first barn.

8 The barn is a beautiful old stone Cumbrian longhouse set on the side of a meadow close to Stonethwaite Beck. Downstairs is a kitchen with microwave, kettle and trestle tables; upstairs is a room with foam mattresses. Sadly there are no straw bales or lambs bleating in cribs: it's all very well-swept.

9 We sleep pretty well. Next morning we bemoan the recent, and permanent, closure of the shop in Rosthwaite—breakfast and lunch will finish all our food supplies.

10 The walk up to Dale Fell takes our minds off this logistical problem: first with all the old slate-mine workings, a fascinating bit of industrial history, then with marvellous views as we hit the ridge, heading west. Far away to our right, across a pack of fells, disappearing in mist, is the Solway Firth; to our left, Morecambe Bay with its wind farms.

1   By the time we drop down into the village of Buttermere, we are tired but happy. It's been a great day's walk. Wilf must have once again done 40 miles to our 10. We are ready to sample either of the two pubs. Our hopes, however, are dashed: both are shut. Recent floods in Cumbria have caused such a dearth of customers that midweek closures have come into force. Cragg Barn is 100 yards up the lane and looks cold. There are snow clouds overhead. Inside is a kitchen —sink and table—then an upstairs sleeping room with foam mattresses wrapped in industrial black plastic. No heating. This is definitely the spartan end of the camping barn experience, and the only food we have is a can of tripe and turkey in gravy, which Wilf refuses to share.

2   There is no mobile coverage so we find a phone box and ring for a taxi. Twenty quid to get back to Keswick for fish and chips; then 20 more to return. If you choose your barn for its proximity to a pub I recommend checking opening times.

3   The final day, and it's the big one. Snow clouds are hovering over Whiteless Breast, our first fell. The views are brief and brilliant: a few seconds of long vistas across sunlight dappled sea to the Isle of Man, swiftly gone. Wilf goes up the slope at top speed and disappears into the cloud, snapping wildly at the first snow flurries of his short life; flurries that are thickening into a white out. We reach the top of Whiteless Pike. I wonder if anyone ever called Mountain Rescue because their dog got lost. At that moment he reappears, only to pursue a snowflake down a steep slope then—horror—over the edge. We all stop.

"Is that a cliff?" asks Con. With visibility at a few metres, it's impossible to tell. The steep grassy bank is slick with ice and snow. I take a couple of tentative steps down. It would be very easy to lose control and slide.

15   At that moment, Wilf scrabbles back over the brink, looking a bit shaken. He bounds back to us, but stays close after that.

16   Conditions are now quite testing. A rising cold wind is driving icy snow into our faces. We push on. This was definitely the rite of passage I had wanted for all my young hounds, but would I be up to it myself? Good trips always have that moment of uncertainty: should we go on? Is it safe?

17   One last challenge is rerouting due to a bridge being washed away, then we are on the path into Keswick where we meet a fellow walker and dog expert who looks Wilf up and down.

18   "Aren't you gorgeous? You're a fell terrier, aren't you?"

19   Wilf seemed to prick up his ears. He was a breed. He was meant to be. We have covered 30 miles and climbed 7,500 feet, but he had done in excess of 100 miles, and, I reckon, scaled a Mount Everest in height. He trotted into Keswick with his tail up, an acknowledged fell terrier. The rest of us were perky also, but in a less demonstrative way. The rite of passage had worked. We were fell terriers, too.

Adapted from an article in "Saturday Guardian"

[END OF PASSAGE]

[BLANK PAGE]

FOR OFFICIAL USE

G

Total
Mark

0860/29/01

NATIONAL
QUALIFICATIONS
2012

THURSDAY, 26 APRIL
1.00 PM – 1.50 PM

ENGLISH
STANDARD GRADE
General Level
Reading
Questions

Fill in these boxes and read what is printed below.

Full name of centre

Town

Forename(s)

Surname

Date of birth

Day   Month   Year   Scottish candidate number   Number of seat

**NB Before leaving the examination room you must give this booklet to the Invigilator.
If you do not, you may lose all the marks for this paper.**

SA 0860/29/01 6/56310

Mar

QUESTIONS

Write your answers in the spaces provided.

Look at Paragraphs 1 and 2.

1. "It's so easy when they're puppies." (Paragraph 1)

   What, according to the writer, is "easy" about caring for a puppy?

   _____

   _____ 2

2. Why is it more difficult to care for an older, bigger dog?

   Use your own words in your answer.

   _____

   _____ 2   1

Look at Paragraphs 3, 4 and 5.

3. ". . . well, let's call it . . ." (Paragraph 3)

   What style of language is the writer using in this expression?

   _____ 2

4. Describe the writer's "vision" of how dogs should behave in pubs and hotels.

   Use your own words in your answer.

   _____

   _____ 2   1

5. "Wilf isn't like that." (Paragraph 5)

   What does Wilf do that isn't "like that"?

   (i) _____

   (ii) _____

   (iii) _____ 2   1

Marks

6. Do the other guests object to Wilf's behaviour? Tick (✓) **one** box.

Yes	
No	

Write down an expression which supports your answer.

_____

2 1 0

7. Identify the contrast between the way Wilf and his owner pass the night in the hotel.

_____

_____

2 1 0

Look at Paragraphs 6 and 7.

8. Why is every hour of daylight "precious"? (Paragraph 6)

_____

_____

2 ■ 0

9. Give **two** reasons why the sheep should be safe from Wilf.

_____

_____

2 1 0

10. Explain how the writer's word choice creates a clear picture of Wilf's behaviour in Paragraph 6.

_____

_____

2 1 0

[Turn over

Mar

Look at Paragraphs 8 and 9.

11.   Identify **three** positive features of the first barn.

(i) _____

(ii) _____

(iii) _____   2 | 1

12.   Explain fully the problem they face the next morning.

_____

_____   2 | 1

Look at Paragraphs 10, 11 and 12.

13.   In what way does the writer contrast the past and the present in Paragraph 10?

_____

_____   2 | 1

14.   Explain **in your own words** the change of mood they experience when they arrive in Buttermere.

_____

_____   2 | 1

15.   Give **two** reasons why Cragg Barn is an uncomfortable place.

_____

_____   2 | 1

Marks

16. The walkers have problems with food in Paragraphs 11 and 12.

　(*a*) Why do they not eat the only tinned food they have left?

　_____   2 ■ 0

　(*b*) Describe the difficulties they face getting fish and chips.

　_____   2 1 0

Look at Paragraphs 13, 14 and 15.

17. The views are "brief and brilliant". (Paragraph 13)

　Identify the technique used in this expression.

　_____   2 ■ 0

18. "Snow clouds are hovering . . ." (Paragraph 13)

　How does the writer show the changing weather conditions in this part of the walk?

　(i) _____

　(ii) _____

　(iii) _____   2 1 0

19. At the end of Paragraph 13, how does the writer use word choice **and** sentence structure to show their panic when Wilf disappears?

　Word choice _____

　Sentence structure _____   2 1 0

[Turn over

PAGE
TOTAL

Mar

20. Which word is closest in meaning to "tentative"? (Paragraph 14)

Tick (✓) **one** answer.

Hurried	
Cautious	
Panicking	
Terrified	

2

Look at Paragraph 16 to the end of the passage.

21. "Conditions are now quite testing." (Paragraph 16)

How does the writer continue this idea later in the passage?

_____

_____

2   1

22. Explain fully why Wilf "seemed to prick up his ears". (Paragraph 19)

_____

_____

2   1

23. Why did the writer feel positive about his family's **and** Wilf's achievements on the walk?

_____

_____

2   1

Marks

Think about the passage as a whole.

24. What seems to be the main purpose of the passage? Tick (✓) **one** box.

To criticise barn camping.	
To give information about the Lake District.	
To describe the challenges they faced on their trip.	

Give **one** piece of evidence to support the answer you have chosen.

_____

2 1 0

[END OF QUESTION PAPER]

PAGE
TOTAL

FOR OFFICIAL USE

p2 ☐

p3 ☐

p4 ☐

p5 ☐

p6 ☐

p7 ☐

TOTAL
MARK ☐

FOR OFFICIAL USE

STANDARD GRADE | FOUNDATION | GENERAL | CREDIT

2008
WRITING

[BLANK PAGE]

**F
G
C**

0860/407

NATIONAL
QUALIFICATIONS
2008

TUESDAY, 6 MAY
9.00 AM – 10.15 AM

ENGLISH
STANDARD GRADE
Foundation, General
and Credit Levels
Writing

Read This First

1   Inside this booklet, there are photographs and words.
Use them to help you when you are thinking about what to write.
Look at all the material and think about all the possibilities.

2   There are 22 assignments altogether for you to choose from.

3   Decide which assignment you are going to attempt.
Choose only **one** and write its number in the margin of your answer book.

4   Pay close attention to what you are asked to write.
Plan what you are going to write.
Read and check your work before you hand it in.
Any changes to your work should be made clearly.

FIRST   **Look at the picture opposite.**
          It shows a car in heavy rain and hail.

NEXT   Think about the dangers of extreme weather.

WHAT YOU HAVE TO WRITE

1. **Write a short story** using the following opening:

    The car skidded violently. He struggled to regain control. Close to panic, he wrenched the steering wheel to the right . . .

    You should develop **setting** and **character** as well as **plot**.

    OR

2. What's going on with our weather?

    Individuals need to take steps to tackle climate change.

    Give your views.

    OR

3. Journeys can take unexpected turns.

    Write about an occasion when this happened to **you**.

    Remember to include your **thoughts and feelings**.

[Turn over

FIRST   **Look at the picture opposite.**
It shows young people together in a school cafeteria.

NEXT   Think about school experiences.

> WHAT YOU HAVE TO WRITE

4. A Best Friend Should Be . . .

    Write about the ideal qualities of a best friend.

OR

5. Youth culture. There's no such thing.

    Give your views.

OR

6. **Write about** an occasion when your loyalty to a friend was pushed to the limit.

    Remember to include your **thoughts and feelings**.

OR

7. **Write a short story** using the following title:

    The School Gate.

    You should develop **setting** and **character** as well as **plot**.

[Turn over

FIRST   **Look at the picture opposite.
It shows a man staring.**

NEXT   Think about being observed.

| WHAT YOU HAVE TO WRITE |
---

8. Big Brother is Watching You!

Write about an occasion when you felt that there was no escape from authority.

Remember to include your **thoughts and feelings**.

OR

9. Write a short story using **ONE** of the following titles:

Seeing is Believing   Close Up

You should develop **setting** and **character** as well as **plot**.

OR

10. All You Need is an Audience.

The media give young people the idea that success comes easily.

Give your views.

[Turn over

FIRST   **Look at the picture opposite.**
         It shows a boy with his grandfather.

NEXT   Think about the positive relationship you have with an older
         relative.

WHAT YOU HAVE TO WRITE

11. **Write about** an occasion when you learned a valuable lesson from
    an older relative.

    Remember to include your **thoughts and feelings**.

    OR

12. **Write a short story** using the following opening:

    Those were the moments he loved most. Grandpa reading to him
    with that lilting voice telling stories of . . .

    You should develop **setting** and **character** as well as **plot**.

    OR

13. We do not give the older generation the respect they deserve.

    Give your views.

    OR

14. **Write in any way you choose** using the picture opposite as your
    inspiration.

[Turn over

FIRST　　**Look at the picture opposite.
It shows an aircraft in the sunset.**

NEXT　　Think about air travel.

| WHAT YOU HAVE TO WRITE |
---

15. The damage to the environment caused by aircraft outweighs the advantages of cheap air travel.

    Give your views.

    OR

16. **Write a short story** using **ONE** of the following titles:

    A New Beginning　　　　　Touchdown

    You should develop **setting** and **character** as well as **plot**.

    OR

17. **Write in any way you choose** using the picture opposite as your inspiration.

[Turn over for assignments 18 to 22 on *Page twelve*

There are no pictures for these assignments.

18. **Write an informative article** for your school magazine titled:

    Technology: the impact on my education.

    OR

19. Nowadays there is less freedom of choice.

    Give your views.

    OR

20. **Write a short story** with the following opening:

    Beth stared again at the square glow from the computer screen in disbelief. She was going to be reunited with her sister at long last. She could hardly wait . . .

    You should develop **setting** and **character** as well as **plot**.

    OR

21. Education is about what we learn both **inside** and **outside** the classroom.

    Give your views.

    OR

22. **Describe the scene** brought to mind by **ONE** of the following:
    EITHER

    Snow fell, the flimsiest drops of geometric perfection, lightly, gently onto the village rooftops.

    OR

    With merciless rage, the sun scorched the earth to brittle hardness.

[END OF QUESTION PAPER]

[BLANK PAGE]

F G C

0860/407

NATIONAL
QUALIFICATIONS
2009

FRIDAY, 8 MAY
9.00 AM – 10.15 AM

ENGLISH
STANDARD GRADE
Foundation, General
and Credit Levels
Writing

Read This First

1 Inside this booklet, there are photographs and words.
Use them to help you when you are thinking about what to write.
Look at all the material and think about all the possibilities.

2 There are 21 assignments altogether for you to choose from.

3 Decide which assignment you are going to attempt.
Choose only **one** and write its number in the margin of your answer book.

4 Pay close attention to what you are asked to write.
Plan what you are going to write.
Read and check your work before you hand it in.
Any changes to your work should be made clearly.

FIRST   **Look at the picture opposite.**
             It shows a statue overlooking a city.

NEXT   Think about life in a city.

WHAT YOU HAVE TO WRITE

---

1. **Write about an occasion** when you went on a school trip to a city.

   Remember to include your **thoughts and feelings**.

   OR

2. Holidays are not just about sun, sea and sand.
   Give your views.

   OR

3. **Write a short story** using the following opening:

   From a great height he watched. Cars, buses, boats, people. Slowly, he drew his plans . . .

   You should develop **setting** and **character** as well as **plot**.

   OR

4. **Write in any way you choose** using the picture opposite as your inspiration.

[Turn over

FIRST   **Look at the pictures opposite.**
                        They show people involved in different sports.

NEXT   Think about what sport means to you.

> ## WHAT YOU HAVE TO WRITE

5. My Sporting Hero.

    Write a magazine article giving information about your favourite sportsperson.

OR

6. There should be more opportunities for sport in local communities.

    Give your views.

OR

7. Write a short story using the title:

    Against the Odds

    You should develop **setting** and **character** as well as **plot**.

OR

8. Write about a sporting occasion when taking part was more important than winning.

    Remember to include your **thoughts and feelings**.

[Turn over

FIRST   **Look at the picture opposite.**
               It shows a tigress and her cubs.

NEXT   Think about protecting animals.

WHAT YOU HAVE TO WRITE

9. One of the Family.

    Write about the importance of a pet in your life.

    Remember to include your **thoughts and feelings**.

OR

10. Write a magazine article in which you present the case **for** the protection of an animal in danger.

OR

11. Write a short story using **ONE** of the following titles:

    The Animal Kingdom   Animal Magic

    You should develop **setting** and **character** as well as **plot**.

[Turn over

FIRST   **Look at the picture opposite.**
         It shows a man at the top of a staircase.

NEXT   Think about achievements in your life.

| WHAT YOU HAVE TO WRITE |

12. **Write about** an occasion when you achieved a personal goal after a struggle.

    Remember to include your **thoughts and feelings**.

    OR

13. Achievement in school is about more than success in exams.
    Give your views.

    OR

14. **Write a short story** using the following opening:

    It had been tough. Sacrifice. Time. Effort. Now she had succeeded. Let the new life begin . . .

    You should develop **setting** and **character** as well as **plot**.

                                                                [Turn over

FIRST   **Look at the picture opposite.**
             It shows two people on a survival course.

NEXT   Think about outdoor activities.

WHAT YOU HAVE TO WRITE

---

15. **Write about** an occasion when you learned new skills through taking part in an outdoor activity.

    Remember to include your **thoughts and feelings**.

OR

16. **Write a short story** using the following title:

    Trapped in the Forest

    You should develop **setting** and **character** as well as **plot**.

OR

17. Outdoor education should be available to all pupils.

    Give your views.

[Turn over for assignments 18 to 21 on *Page twelve*

There are no pictures for these assignments.

18. **Describe the scene** brought to mind by **ONE** of the following:

   Light as air, they hovered then swooped, twisting impossibly around feather clouds.

   OR

   Waves lapped at pebbles on the distant shore and a kindly sun drew a gentle haze over the land.

19. Holidays at home are better for the environment than going abroad.

   Give your views.

   OR

20. **Write about** an occasion when you were a positive role model for a friend or relative.

   Remember to include your **thoughts and feelings**.

   OR

21. **Write a short story** using the following title:

   Paradise Lost

   You should develop **setting** and **character** as well as **plot**.

[END OF QUESTION PAPER]

[BLANK PAGE]

**F
G
C**

0860/407

NATIONAL
QUALIFICATIONS
2010

THURSDAY, 29 APRIL
9.00 AM – 10.15 AM

ENGLISH
STANDARD GRADE
Foundation, General
and Credit Levels
Writing

Read This First

1   Inside this booklet, there are photographs and words.
Use them to help you when you are thinking about what to write.
Look at all the material and think about all the possibilities.

2   There are 21 assignments altogether for you to choose from.

3   Decide which assignment you are going to attempt.
Choose only **one** and write its number in the margin of your answer book.

4   Pay close attention to what you are asked to write.
Plan what you are going to write.
Read and check your work before you hand it in.
Any changes to your work should be made clearly.

FIRST   **Look at the picture opposite.**
               It shows a woman on a skateboard being helped by an
               expert.

NEXT   Think about new challenges.

| WHAT YOU HAVE TO WRITE |

---

1. **Write a short story** using the title:

   The Rebel

   You should develop **setting** and **character** as well as **plot**.

   OR

2. We all have hidden talents.

   Education should be about discovering our strengths, not our weaknesses.

   Give your views.

   OR

3. **Write about** an occasion when you had an experience that changed your life.

   Remember to include your **thoughts and feelings**.

   OR

4. Look on the Bright Side!

   We need to have a more positive outlook on life.

   Give your views.

FIRST   **Look at the picture opposite.
It shows an example of street art.**

NEXT   Think about expressing yourself.

WHAT YOU HAVE TO WRITE

5. Graffiti: art or vandalism?
    Give your views.

    OR

6. **Write about** an occasion when breaking a rule was more important than following it.
    Remember to include your **thoughts and feelings**.

    OR

7. **Write a short story** using the title:
    The Smile
    You should develop **setting** and **character** as well as **plot**.

    [Turn over

FIRST   **Look at the picture opposite.**
             It shows a fairground at night.

NEXT   Think about the attraction of fairgrounds.

WHAT YOU HAVE TO WRITE

---

8. **Write a short story** using the following opening:

   Sal awakened slowly. Dazed at first, she tried to focus but she was still dizzy from the rollercoaster. At last, her eyes fixed on the empty booth, then beyond to the empty stalls and the empty fairground . . .

   You should develop **setting** and **character** as well as **plot**.

   OR

9. Entertainment today is too expensive for many young people.

   Give your views.

   OR

10. Fun for Everyone!

    Describe your favourite fairground attraction.

    Remember to include your **thoughts and feelings**.

                                                        [Turn over

FIRST **Look at the pictures opposite.**
       They show images of Scotland.

NEXT   Think about living in Scotland.

WHAT YOU HAVE TO WRITE

11. **Write about** an occasion when you took part in a Scottish celebration or festival.

    Remember to include your **thoughts and feelings**.

    OR

12. **Write an article** for your school magazine in which you argue the case either **for** or **against** an independent Scotland.

    OR

13. **Write a short story** using the following opening:

    From the darkness, a glimmering light sparked faintly and began to glow . . .

    You should develop **setting** and **character** as well as **plot**.

[Turn over

FIRST   **Look at the picture opposite.**
                It shows two long shadows.

NEXT   Think about darkness and light.

WHAT YOU HAVE TO WRITE

14. **Write a short story** using the following opening:

    Something just wasn't right. He turned. Nothing. He turned again to see the outline of a dark figure . . .

    You should develop **setting** and **character** as well as **plot**.

    OR

15. Always in their Shadow!

    Write about an occasion when you felt second best.

    Remember to include your **thoughts and feelings**.

    OR

16. **Write in any way you choose** using the picture opposite as your inspiration.

[Turn over for assignments 17 to 21 on *Page twelve*

There are no pictures for these assignments.

17. **Describe the scene** brought to mind by **one** of the following:

    Rain stained the still warm path; each collision a hiss.

    OR

    Slowly the sun dawned on an endless golden land.

    OR

18. **Write an article** for your school magazine **describing** a visit to an unusual or interesting building.

    OR

19. **Write about** an occasion when you were given good advice but did not take it.

    Remember to include your **thoughts and feelings**.

    OR

20. **Write a short story** using the following title:

    The Arrival

    OR

21. Learning to drive. Managing your money. Parenting.

    What life skills would you like to learn at school?

[END OF QUESTION PAPER]

[BLANK PAGE]

F
G
C

0860/407

NATIONAL
QUALIFICATIONS
2011

FRIDAY, 6 MAY
9.00 AM – 10.15 AM

ENGLISH
STANDARD GRADE
Foundation, General
and Credit Levels
Writing

Read This First

1   Inside this booklet, there are photographs and words.
     Use them to help you when you are thinking about what to write.
     Look at all the material and think about all the possibilities.

2   There are 20 assignments altogether for you to choose from.

3   Decide which assignment you are going to attempt.
     Choose only **one** and write its number in the margin of your answer book.

4   Pay close attention to what you are asked to write.
     Plan what you are going to write.
     Read and check your work before you hand it in.
     Any changes to your work should be made clearly.

FIRST **Look at the picture opposite.**
It shows an anxious young man on his mobile phone.

NEXT Think about difficult situations.

WHAT YOU HAVE TO WRITE

1. **Write a short story** using the following opening:

   Life was wonderful. Just great. Paul didn't have a care in the world. It was then that the phone rang . . .

   You should develop **setting** and **character** as well as **plot**.

   OR

2. **Write about** an occasion when **you** had a telephone call giving you unwelcome news.

   Remember to include your **thoughts and feelings**.

   OR

3. Stress. Stress. Stress. It's all we seem to hear these days.

   Some stress is actually good for people.

   Give your views.

[Turn over

FIRST   **Look at the picture opposite.**
         It shows a boat in a storm.

NEXT   Think about risks and dangers.

WHAT YOU HAVE TO WRITE
---

4. **Write a short story** using **one** of the following titles:

    Overboard   The Boat

    You should develop **setting** and **character** as well as **plot**.

    OR

5. Everyday life is full of risks. We can't avoid them.

    We simply need to accept that life is a risk.

    Give your views.

    OR

6. **Write about** an occasion when you took a memorable journey by boat.

    Remember to include your **thoughts and feelings.**

    OR

7. **Write in any way you choose** using the picture opposite as your inspiration.

                                                    [Turn over

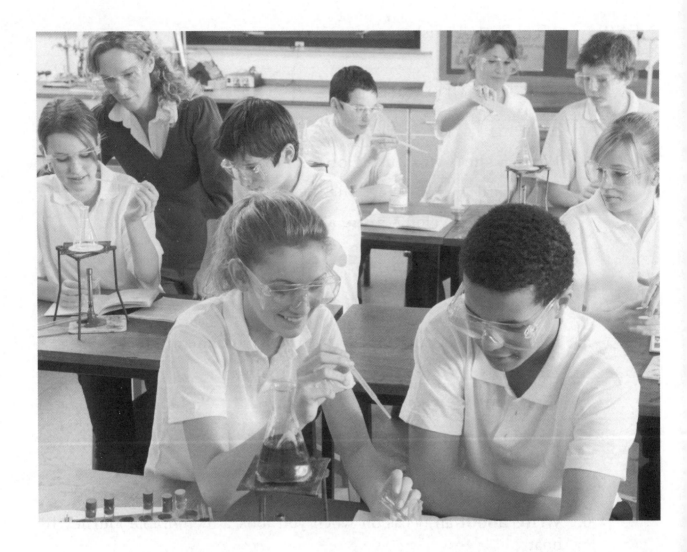

FIRST   **Look at the picture opposite.**
It shows a science lesson.

NEXT   Think about science and technology.

WHAT YOU HAVE TO WRITE

8. It is important that all pupils study science at school.
   Give your views.

   OR

9. **Write a short story** using **one** of the following titles:

   The Experiment   The Monster

   You should develop **setting** and **character** as well as **plot.**

   OR

10. **Write about** an occasion when science **or** technology changed your life.

   Remember to include your **thoughts and feelings**.

[Turn over

FIRST   **Look at the picture opposite.**
                 It shows a bookshop.

NEXT   Think about the importance of reading.

WHAT YOU HAVE TO WRITE

---

11. **Write a short story** using the following opening:

     She entered and walked to the back of the shop. She counted the bookshelves. One. Two. Three. This was it. She removed the book. And found herself in . . .

     You should develop **setting** and **character** as well as **plot.**

     OR

12. Reading books on a screen will never replace the good old-fashioned paperback.

     Give your views.

     OR

13. Curled up in front of the fire with a good book. Perfect.

     Write about the pleasure reading gives **you**.

     Remember to include your **thoughts and feelings.**

[Turn over

FIRST   **Look at the picture opposite.
             It shows children playing at sunset.**

NEXT   Think about childhood memories.

WHAT YOU HAVE TO WRITE

14. **Write about** an occasion when you enjoyed a childhood pleasure.
    Remember to include your **thoughts and feelings.**

    OR

15. **Write a short story** using the title:
    Sunset

    You should develop **setting** and **character** as well as **plot**.

    OR

16. **Write in any way you choose** using the picture opposite as your
    inspiration.

[Turn over for assignments 17 to 20 on *Page twelve*

There are no pictures for these assignments.

17. **Describe the scene** brought to mind by **one** of the following:

    EITHER

    Ice. Endless blue ice for a hundred miles in any direction. Sharp, cold, beautiful.

    OR

    Gold. Endless golden fields stretching and swaying in gentle winds to the far horizons.

    OR

18. **Write a description** of your local park.

    OR

19. We need more green spaces in cities.
    Give your views.

    OR

20. **Write a short story** using the title:

    Escape from the City

    You should develop **setting** and **character** as well as **plot**.

[END OF QUESTION PAPER]

STANDARD GRADE | FOUNDATION | GENERAL | CREDIT

2012
WRITING

[BLANK PAGE]

**F
G
C**

0860/32/01

NATIONAL THURSDAY, 26 APRIL ENGLISH
QUALIFICATIONS 9.00 AM – 10.15 AM STANDARD GRADE
2012 Foundation, General
and Credit Levels
Writing

Read This First

1 Inside this booklet, there are photographs and words.
   Use them to help you when you are thinking about what to write.
   Look at all the material and think about all the possibilities.

2 There are 23 assignments altogether for you to choose from.

3 Decide which assignment you are going to attempt.
   Choose only **one** and write its number in the margin of your answer book.

4 Pay close attention to what you are asked to write.
   Plan what you are going to write.
   Read and check your work before you hand it in.
   Any changes to your work should be made clearly.

FIRST   **Look at the picture opposite.**
          It shows a man surrounded by gadgets.

NEXT   Think about our need for possessions.

WHAT YOU HAVE TO WRITE

---

1. Our lives today are too cluttered. The pressure on us to buy new
    things increases daily.

    Give your views.

    OR

2. Buy. Buy. Buy.

    Write about an occasion when you felt the need to buy something
    new.

    Remember to include your **thoughts and feelings**.

    OR

3. **Write a short story** using the following title:

    The Treasure Hunt

    You should develop **setting** and **character** as well as **plot**.

[Turn over

FIRST   **Look at the picture opposite.**
        It shows an old, ruined house.

NEXT   Think about the effects of time passing.

| WHAT YOU HAVE TO WRITE |

4. **Write a description** of the scene suggested by the picture opposite.

    OR

5. There are many lessons we can learn from the past.
    Give your views.

    OR

6. **Write about** an occasion when you made a fresh start.
    Remember to include your **thoughts and feelings**.

    OR

7. **Write an informative article** for your school magazine in which you describe a visit to a place of historic interest.

[Turn over

FIRST   **Look at the picture opposite.**
         It shows a violinist.

NEXT   Think about performing.

WHAT YOU HAVE TO WRITE

---

8. **Write about** the importance of musical performance to **you**.

    Remember to include your **thoughts and feelings**.

    OR

9. **Write a short story** using the following opening:

    She caught her breath, then anxiously took to the stage. Blinding light. Deafening applause. She began . . .

    You should develop **setting** and **character** as well as **plot**.

    OR

10. Becoming really good at something always involves hard work.

    Give your views.

[Turn over

Image taken from www.bigfoto.com

FIRST   **Look at the picture opposite.**
         It shows people playing in the snow.

NEXT   Think about winter.

WHAT YOU HAVE TO WRITE

---

11. Unexpected Fun.

     Write about an occasion when your school was closed because of the weather.

     Remember to include your **thoughts and feelings**.

     OR

12. **Write a short story** using the following opening:

     One by one, slowly, the children began to gather in the snow-filled park . . .

     You should develop **setting** and **character** as well as **plot**.

     OR

13. Winter is the best season of all.

     Give your views.

     OR

14. **Write in any way you choose** using the picture opposite as your inspiration.

[Turn over

FIRST   **Look at the picture opposite.**
           It shows a biker performing a stunt.

NEXT   Think about sports and pastimes.

| WHAT YOU HAVE TO WRITE |

15. **Write an informative article** for a magazine about an interesting sport or pastime.

    OR

16. **Write a short story** using the following title:

    No Fear

    You should develop **setting** and **character** as well as **plot**.

    OR

17. **Write about** an occasion when **preparing** for a competition was as important as the competition itself.

    Remember to include your **thoughts and feelings**.

    OR

18. It's just not worth it.

    Extreme sports are simply too risky.

    Give your views.

[Turn over for assignments 19 to 23 on *Page twelve*

There are no pictures for these assignments.

19. **Describe the scene** brought to mind by **ONE** of the following:

> *On the tall peaks the glistening sunbeams play,*
> *With a light heart our course we may renew,*
> *The first whose footsteps print the mountain dew.*

OR

> *In flakes of light upon the mountain side;*
> *Where with loud voice the power of water shakes*
> *The leafy wood, or sleeps in quiet lakes.*
>
> William Wordsworth

OR

20. We are all different, so we all learn differently.

There are now lots of opportunities to learn in ways suited to the individual.

Give your views.

OR

21. My Dream Destination.

Write about the one place in the world you would really like to visit.

OR

22. We are a society motivated by money.

Give your views.

OR

23. **Write a short story** using the following title:

The High Life

You should develop **setting** and **character** as well as **plot**.

[END OF QUESTION PAPER]

[BLANK PAGE]

Acknowledgements

Permission has been sought from all relevant copyright holders and Bright Red Publishing is grateful for the use of the following:

An extract from 'Home for Christmas' taken from a book called 'Mysterious Christmas Tales' by David Belbin. Published by Scholastic. Reproduced with permission of Jennifer Luithlen Agency (2008 Foundation Close Reading pages 2 & 3);

The article 'Saddle the white horses' by Dave Flanagan, taken from The Herald magazine 22 April 2006 © David Flanagan (2008 General Close Reading page 2);

A photograph taken from www.bigfoto.com (2008 F/G/C Writing page 2);

The photograph 'Chips are down' by Robert Perry taken from Scotland on Sunday, 2 July 2006 © The Scotsman Publications Ltd (2008 F/G/C Writing page 4);

The photograph 'Eye Opener' © Steve Double (2008 F/G/C Writing page 6);

The photograph 'Language Lesson' © Julie Brook (2008 F/G/C Writing page 8);

The photograph 'Airbus 320' by Ian Britton. Reproduced with permission of Freefoto.com (2008 F/G/C Writing page 10);

An extract from 'Crocodile River' by Geoffrey Malone, published by Hodder Children's Books (2000) (2009 Foundation Close Reading pages 2 & 3);

An extract from 'Labyrinth' by Kate Mosse, published by Orion Books, an imprint of the Orion Publishing Group, London (2009 General Close Reading pages 2 & 3);

A photograph taken from www.bigfoto.com (2009 F/G/C Writing page 2);

A photograph © FRANCK FIFE/AFP/Getty Images (2009 F/G/C Writing page 4);

A photograph by Phil Wilkinson © The Scotsman Publications Ltd (2009 F/G/C Writing page 4);

The photograph 'Surfing. Saltburn by the Sea, Yorkshire' by Ian Britton. Reproduced with permission of Freefoto.com (2009 F/G/C Writing page 4);

A photograph of a girl ski-ing © Neil McQuoid (2009 F/G/C Writing page 4);

A photograph © Blackout Concepts/Alamy (2009 F/G/C Writing page 8);

The photograph 'I will survive: Learning to make fire without matches is a basic bushcraft skill © Roger Bamber/Alamy (2009 F/G/C Writing page 10);

An extract from 'Things in Corners' by Ruth Park, published by Penguin Books Australia, 1989 © Ruth Park (2010 Foundation Close Readiing pages 2 & 3);

The article 'Chimps Go Ape In Zoo' by Adam Forrest, taken from 'The Big Issue' Magazine, May 1–7 2008 © The Big Issue (2010 General Close Reading page 2);

The photograph 'Pensioner with a skateboarding expert' © Newsquest (Herald & Times). Licensor www.scran.ac.uk (2010 F/G/C Writing page 2);

The photograph 'A street artist and his chalk drawing' © Marius Alexander. Licensor www.scran.ac.uk (2010 F/G/C Writing page 4);

A photograph © George Clerk/iStockphoto (2010 F/G/C Writing page 8);

The photograph 'Big Wheel' © Newsquest (Herald & Times). Licensor www.scran.ac.uk (2010 F/G/C Writing page 6);

The photograph 'Exterior of the Scottish Parliament Holyrood Building by night' © Scottish Parliament. Licensor www.scran.ac.uk (2010 F/G/C Writing page 8);

The photograph 'The aqueduct and boat lift, Falkirk Wheel, 2002' © Falkirk Museums. Licensor www.scran.ac.uk (2010 F/G/C Writing page 8);

The photograph 'Autumn ground shot with strewn leaves and long shadows' © Jack Stevenson. Licensor www.scran.ac.uk (2010 F/G/C Writing page 10);

An extract from 'The Iron Woman' by Ted Hughes, published by Faber and Faber (2011 Foundation Reading pages 2 & 3);

The article 'Bright Lights Big City' by Janice Galloway, taken from The Sunday Herald Magazine, 2008 © Janice Galloway (2011 General Reading pages 2 & 3);

Two photographs © Herald & Times Group (2011 General Reading page 2);

A photograph © Martin Lee/Rex Images (2011 F/G/C Writing page 2);

A photograph © Adam Lau (2011 F/G/C Writing page 4);

A photograph © Catherine Yeulet/iStockphoto (2011 F/G/C Writing page 6);

A photograph © Daniel Yee (2011 F/G/C Writing page 8);

'Black mamba' article taken from BBC Wildlife Magazine, November 2009 by Thea Litschka © Immediate Media Company Bristol Limited (2012 Foundation Reading page 2);

An article and two photographs by Kevin Rushby, taken from the travel section of 'Saturday Guardian' 23 January 2010. Copyright Guardian News & Media Ltd 2010 (2012 General Reading page 2);

Photograph of Balgownie Mill, Eassie, By Glamis. Presently owned by Mr C Heath, image © Bell Ingram Design, who are converting the existing mill into a dwelling house (2012 F/G/C Writing page 4);

Image taken from www.bigfoto.com (2012 F/G/C Writing page 8).

STANDARD GRADE | ANSWER SECTION

SQA STANDARD GRADE
FOUNDATION AND GENERAL ENGLISH
2008–2012

ENGLISH FOUNDATION
READING 2008

1. **when**: Christmas Eve
   where: (motorway) services/petrol station

2. *Any two from:*

   (i) (nearly) five hours

   (ii) • without (a sniff of) a lift
   • no one had (even) slowed down
   • weather was lousy
   • he'd dozed off

3. (i) (getting) dark

   (ii) Fog (was coming in)

4. "drove by him"/"as if he wasn't there"

5. Small/could fit under his legs

6. • it contained all he had

   • used to belong to his mum

7. (*a*) • to get a bed
   • something to eat

   (*b*) • (probably get) run over
   • reference to luck alone

8. (*a*) Cough / had a cold for two months/a long time

   (*b*) Sleeping rough for a year/a long time

9. (i) Warm up

   (ii) Get cup of coffee

10. "presuming they'd serve him"/"he looked a mess"

11. (i) Shivering (due to cold)
    (ii) Wet through/reference to jacket not keeping him dry
    (iii) Puddles around his feet

12. Not really shower-proof
    OR accept reference to manufacturer's
    claim/advertising/written on jacket etc

13. (i) Lights not on

    (ii) Close to kerb

14. (*a*)

rhyme	
metaphor	
alliteration	
simile	✓

   (*b*) (i) He cannot see (clearly)
   (ii) Helpless/cannot or does not move/afraid/stunned or
   similar

15. Billy cannot see him
    Reference to deep voice/harsh voice

16. (i) Driver is Scottish (like himself)/driver has Scottish accent
    (like his)
    (ii) Driver can take him (all the way) home

17. Billy no longer feels that it is home/Billy is no longer sure that
    it is home/Billy uncertain about his reception or similar/Billy
    misses his home

18. Reference to cold/winter
    Reference to miserable/unwelcoming

19.

a conversation	
a gadget	
a way of behaving correctly	✓
a solution to a problem	

20. *Any three from:*

   (i) Silence

   (ii) Brief responses

   (iii) • interruption
   • does not want music
   • way he speaks
   • drives faster

21. He is not having a good time so he feels (even) worse/jealous
    OR if you are not having a good time you feel (even) worse

22. For "yes" accept any two suitable references such as:

   • homeless

   • unwell

   • no one to care for him

   • possibly in danger

   • afraid of Hank

   • hint of family problems

   • hardly any possessions

   • cold

   • wet

   For "no" accept any two suitable references such as:

   • he does get a lift at the end

   • he is going home

   • might have run away from home

   • possibly stole rucksack from mum

ENGLISH GENERAL
READING 2008

1. (a) (surfing) stickers

   (b) *Any two from*:
   • Thurso 23 miles away
   • have taken the right turn-off (for Thurso)
   • nearly at their destination

2. Short paragraph/one sentence paragraph
   OR reference to word choice "big league" suggests dramatic or similar

3. (a) Gloss of "tropical" eg hot/exotic/beach with palm trees

   (b) "raw"/"exposed"/"worst excesses of the Scottish climate"

4. The best (of all the Caithness surfing spots)

5. Reference to speed/power/ferocity/frightening/
   danger/(rolling) movement/size/shape
   (*Any two*)

6. (i) (first time) held in Scotland

   (ii) Furthest north it has been held

7. WCT gloss of "premier division" eg best competitors/
          higher status
   WQS gloss of "platform … to move up into the big time"
          eg step towards the better competition accept reference
          to lower status

8. (i) Reference to prize money

   (ii) (vital tour) points

9. (i) (enjoy) travelling/new place/adventure/new experience

   (ii) One of the best waves in Europe/big reef break waves

   (iii) Reference to photographs (*any three*)

10. Cold/harsh conditions

    OR reference to "Thurso is one of the best waves in Europe, if
       not the world."

11. Big/dramatic/exciting waves
    OR reference to challenging weather conditions
    OR reference to contrast with tropical events

12. They don't want/to protect from/to stop (or similar)
    overcrowding (or similar)

13. Informal/chatty/slang or similar

14. (i) Met surfers/addressed their concerns

    (ii) Paid for car park improvements

15. "most of them are positive" must have whole expression

16. boycott

17. (a)

negative and angry	
quite pleased but worried	
excited and not really anxious	✓

   (b) *Any one from:*
   • "eagerly anticipating"
   • "makes me feel proud"
   • "don't think it's going to be that bad"
   • "doesn't anticipate a negative impact"
   • "it'll generate business for us"

18. (Thurso is) far away/unknown/like another world

19. (a) Negative: gloss of "live out of your bag a lot" eg
        few comforts/few belongings with you/never in one place
        for long/gloss of "long stints away from home" eg not at
        home for long periods of time

    (b) Positive: reference to seeing many/varied/new places OR
        gloss of "perform well" eg (competition) success OR gloss
        of "get some really good waves" eg good conditions/exciting
        surf/waves just right

20. (i) Length of ride

    (ii) Difficulty of moves

    (iii) How they connect it all together

21. (i)

to tell the reader some amusing stories about surfing	
to inform the reader about a surfing competition in Scotland	✓
to argue against holding a surfing competition in Scotland	

    (ii) Accept appropriate reference to information in the passage
    eg
    • surfing/the life of a surfer/the competition scoring
      system
    • Thurso as a surfing location/the WQS and WCT

ENGLISH FOUNDATION READING 2009

1. camping/outdoor adventure

2. "glided"

3. large: "boulders"/"(huge) flowers"/"lily pads (a metre wide)"

 colourful: "(white) boulders"/"(purple) flowers"/"(bright green) ferns"

4. *Any three from:*
sweating/sweat-stained/hot/tired/sand in hair/sand under nails/sand in shorts/sand everywhere

5. (*a*) simile

 (*b*) reference to smooth/soft/cool/pleasant

6. relaxing/peaceful/pleasant/stress disappearing

7. Sam shouting/interrupting

8. (i) he did: grabbed Tom's arm/dragged Tom away/scowled/hissed/put his face into Tom's

 (ii) he said: "What the heck you doing?"/"You want to see your mother again?"/"You want to get me into big trouble?"/"You think you know better than me?"

9. he forgot to tell him/did not tell him about the crocodiles

10. reference to "had a really good look"
reference to "nothing there"

11. *Any two from:*
reference to "hide"/"watch"/"waiting"/"all day"/"don't miss a trick"/surprise/sudden attack

12. shock/horror/surprise/reference to deaths

13. (i) no man can outrun crocodile/if crocodile chases you, you will die

 (ii) can run at 20 miles an hour (over 50m)

14. Sam's bed
he (ie Sam) sleeps on ground

15. learn about them

16. lots of them/spilling out/danger/anger/fast/sudden movement/like a liquid

17. *Any two from:*
reference to pain/puncturing skin or biting/number of bites or ants

18. reference to "he thought it a great joke"

19. (more) dangerous/not safe (like park)

20. dug a hole (for fire)

21. *Any two from:*
reference to lethal eg if place catches fire they'll die/ reference to spreading eg might start bush fire/ reference to height eg wall of fire metres high/ reference to speed eg spreads faster than can drive OR in a couple of minutes

22. short/reference to alliteration/focus on important words/non-sentence/end of paragraph

23. same as his grandmother used/used back home in more adventurous setting/strange setting expected Greg to rub sticks together

24. (i) if terrifying, reference to crocodiles/ant attack/bush fire/snakes
if exciting, reference to paddling in river/seeing new sights/making a fire/threat of crocodiles/encountering ants

 (ii) if embarrassing, reference to mistake about crocodiles/disturbing ants/not knowing about fire/knows less than the others/reaction of others

ENGLISH GENERAL
READING 2009

1. (historical) dig/archaeology

2. danger/problem/difficulty
   linked to job

3. *Any three from*
   Alice is thirsty/drink is warmed up
   heat haze/blue sky

4. (*a*) list (of activities)

   (*b*) "digging"/"scraping"/"cataloguing"/"recording"/ (use of)
   verbs

5. "demoralised"/"little to justify their efforts"/"only a few
   fragments"/"couple of arrowheads"

6. *Any two from:*
   tired/sore legs/sore shoulders/reference to lack of
   success/reference to colleagues taking a break

7.
She wants to show that she can do the job herself	True
She does not like her colleagues.	Cannot tell
She wants to share her discovery.	False

8. (*a*) "(flutter of) excitement"

   (*b*) "(knows) she's got something worth finding"/"telling
   herself not to expect too much"

9. to emphasise care/slowness

10. absorbed

11. *Any two from*
    "so absorbed"/"doesn't notice"/"world seems to hang
    suspended"/"mesmerised"

12. big OR heavy stone not (normally) graceful

13. reference to alliteration

14. realises (gloss of "it sinks in") she nearly died or
    "how very close she came to being crushed" (gloss of "how
    very close she came to being crushed")

15. reference to opening in mountain
    distracts her/curiosity/drawn towards it/wants to keep it to
    herself

16. *Any two from*
    big/strong/prevents people going in the entrance/keeps cave
    and contents safe/reference to personification

17. reference to "(velvet) black" becoming "(charcoal) grey"
    reference to sees tunnel/can see what lies ahead

18. (i) anxious/scared

    (ii) feels she is doing something wrong

19. *Any two from:*
    short/paragraph on its own/reference to "abruptly" eg sudden
    change in her feelings/cliffhanger OR
    makes reader want to know what happened next

20. makes you feel it is happening now/feel you're there as it's
    happening/makes you feel involved

21. (i) if 'return to colleagues' accept references to growing
    feelings that she should seek help/her injuries/frightening
    situation/desire to show colleagues the buckle

    (ii) if 'go further in' accept references to something drawing
    her in/excited about buckle/adventurous/
    determined/independent
    if 'trapped' accept references to something drawing her
    in/unease at end/eeriness of cave/falling stone

ENGLISH FOUNDATION READING 2010

1. he became ill
   for several weeks (in bed)

2. boring   disagreeable

3. *Any three from:*
   "fever"
   "aches"
   "wobbliness"/ref. to "damp grey curtain"

4. (a) *Any two from:*
   "sharp"/"stringy"/"always on the go"/"interested in most things"/"ready to do something about them"/"fearless"
   (b) (now) didn't much care for anything

5. Theo's dad has a new job/promotion/reference to manager

6.

Suspicious	
Thrilled	✓
Angry	
Pleased	

7. Feeling: happy/excited or similar
   Evidence: ref. to "smile"/ "sunshine"/"kept interrupting"/"running to the window"/ "blissfully crying"/"I can see the river"/ "Oh Ted"/"I can see the lovely hills"/ "I've always wanted hills"/ "And the smell of everything in here, Ted"/"all new and clean and painty" Lift or gloss acceptable

8. There were some things he did not like about his father or similar

9. (i) "parents so happy"/"he was happy"
   (ii) new home

10. (i) "fifth floor"
    (ii) "legs rickety"
    (iii) "odd sensation in his stomach"

11. (a) *Any two from:*
    "wasteland"/"raw soil"/"willows sticking up"/"funny-shaped area"/"dry (sabre) leaves"/ "leaves edged in yellow"/"concrete"
    (b) "time would fix that"

12. (a)

Metaphor	
Rhyme	
Alliteration	
Simile	✓

    (b) sharp/cutting/cold

13. (i) "he had been indoors more than a month"
    (ii) "year had moved on"/"soon it would be winter"

14. (i) "smelled of varnish"
    (ii) "new rubber flooring"

15. "(he saw it) pulsing (slowly)"

16. short (sentence)/first sentence (in the paragraph)

17. *Any three from:*
    "formless"/"three-quarters-set"/"(faint) sheen"/ "grey"/"wet-looking"/ "blob"/"melted"

18. *Any two from:*
    misery/helplessness/   shudder/quiver

19. he collapsed/fell/became ill or similar

20. fussing or similar

21. "couldn't have seen that thing"/impossible for it to exist/too strange/he was ill

22. *Any two appropriate reasons from:*
    if " ... will go back to the lift ... " accept reference to "sharp"/"always on the go"/ "interested"/ "fearless" /uncertainty about experience etc.
    if " ... will try to forget ... " accept reference to horrifying experience/Theo's
    physical weakness/desire to enjoy new start in house/conviction he had not seen it etc.
    if "... will tell his mum ..." accept reference to close family/ caring parents/Theo too weak to deal with it alone etc.

ENGLISH GENERAL
READING 2010

1. *Any two from:*
   outside/on the other side of the glass from chimp enclosure at the zoo

2. *Any two from:*
   (i) eating boiled egg/
   (ii) travelling in ship/reference to "snooty gesture"

3. *Any two from:*
   reference to stops what he is doing/reference to change in facial expression/reference to goes back to eating

4. *Any three from:*
   (i) enclosure "state-of-the-art"/"air-conditioned"/ "cost 5.6 million pounds"/
   (ii) "luxury"/"largest chimp enclosure in the world"/
   (iii) "higher standard of living than most humans"

5. active: "longest"
   or "(most) intricate climbing frame"
   safe: moat

6. ordinary/house   (millionaire's) mansion

7. they can study the chimps
   in environment similar to the wild

8. Proud   gloss of "he helped design" enclosure eg involved in planning
   Delighted   gloss of "realised so spectacularly" eg worked out so well/dream came true
               or reference to public reaction

9. *Any two from:*
   "(cartoon) game"/"children learn chimp gestures"/
   "kids will be running around, touching everything"

10.
Rather uninterested	
Very enthusiastic	✓
Slightly critical	

   He was model for cartoon game/he demonstrates chimp movements for writer/reference to "as they should"

11. Link with conservation work/research into threats to chimps in the Budongo Forest/Uganda

12. Gloss of "habitat destruction" eg homes disappearing
    Gloss of "traps set for bush meat" eg hunted for food

13.
To study closely	
To help	
To relate to	
To tell apart	✓

14. (*a*) "personalities"/reference to personality traits
         "(glossy monthly) magazine"
    (*b*) to get people interested in them/to identify with them/to attract visitors

15. alliteration

16. he could become leader
    too young/thin (just now)/still learning things

17. (*a*) eating on his own/mixing with humans/reference to lack of interaction with other chimps
    (*b*) reference to grooming (a bit more)

18. (i)   reference to size/height of enclosure
    (ii) reference to soil
    (iii) reference to behaviour

19. their language varies
    in different places

20. gloss of "fresh marvels" eg new discoveries or similar
    gloss of "daily basis" eg every day/regularly/always or similar

21. reference to watching chimps eg "noting the quirks of the Budongo 11"
    reference to communicating with chimps eg "say hello"

22. (i)   appropriate for/sums up subject matter
    (ii) "go ape" suggests extreme behaviour

23.
To argue that animals like chimps should not be kept in zoos	
To give a positive, informative view of the new enclosure	✓
To request donations for the upkeep of the new enclosure	

   reference to positive feature of enclosure eg comfort/activities/size/link to conservation work

ENGLISH FOUNDATION READING 2011

1. Where marsh road/between reed banks/way home (from school)/(Otterfeast)Bridge
   When after school/(start of) Easter Holidays

2. she had seen an otter
   eating an eel

3. excitement eagerly

4. *Any two from:*
   ref to "peered"/"something"/question/"What was it?"/"A fish?"

5. *Any two from:*
   like "two eels fighting"/"knotted itself"/"unknotted"/"swam quickly round in circles"/"corkscrewing over and over"/"tail flipped"/"writhing down into mud"/"bobbing its head"/"little mouth opening"

6. disturbing the water so much/so much movement or similar

7. *Any two from:*
   ref to wriggling/round and round/speed/rhythm/changing direction

8. surfaces/appears repeatedly

9. (*a*) ref to emotional response eg sympathy/concern
      OR ref to physical response: "painful twist (somewhere in her middle)"

   (*b*) scoop it up/help it

10. (i) gripped the bridge/rails
    (ii) braced her feet apart

11. short/paragraph on its own

12. sound made by heron
    or (to show) heron frightened

13. *Any one from:*
    floppy/untidy/flailed/hoisted/tumbled

14. ref to heron behaviour/eel gone/scared/strange things happening

15. *Any three from:*
    sky/clouds/water/reeds/"whorls of light"

16. *Any two from:*
    bridge or road moves/rail moves/ripples on water

17. greater/different (fear than before)

18.

Metaphor	
Simile	
Rhyme	
Alliteration	✓

19. *Any two from:*
    unsteady/moving
    high up
    ref to danger/Lucy's fear

20. *Any two from:*
    ceiling of house falling on mother/village flattened/machinery toppling on father

21. strength of shocks/earthquake

22. "Nothing like any bird"/"long wailing cry"/"like a fire engine siren"/uses simile

23. any suitable ref eg naming bridge/bridge's unsteadiness/disappearing into middle of the earth/parents' fate/village's fate

24. *Any two appropriate reasons from:*
    if "rush back home": refs to fear for herself/concern for parents/concern for village/knows area
    if "get lost": refs to panic/earthquake/disorientation/"blindly"

ENGLISH GENERAL
READING 2011

1. special link with Christmas/identified Glasgow with Christmas/ when she thought of Glasgow she thought of Christmas/ important event/or similar idea

2. lived at seaside   did not swim
   OR appreciated beauty   broke ornaments

3. alliteration/list

4. *Any three from:*
   dazzle/warmth of crowds/(snowy) shop displays/cheer/ hundreds of trees/lights

5. Did "rolling her eyes"
   Said "Our town is a dump"/"(We've only a) daft wee tree"

6. *Any two from:*
   ref to made to dress up/mother cleaning her face with spit or hurting her face/warning her about gloves

7. paragraph on its own/sentence on its own/short sentence

8. could see very little (gloss of "our view was strips"/"visible in glimpses") due to dirty windows (gloss of "filthy"/"through grime")

9. *Any two from:*
   "big enough for trains to roll right inside"/"high as cliffs"/"pigeons indoors"/"clock the size of our bathroom" lift or gloss acceptable

10. *Any two from:*
    (*a*) metaphor/simile/alliteration/assonance
    (*b*) flying up/flying away/taking off/spreading their wings

11. *Any two from:*
    "(buildings coated in velvet-deep) soot"/"charcoal-coloured (statues)"/"ash-grey (walls)"/general comment on dirty or dark features

12. "my face brushing against the tweedy coats of strangers"

13. parenthesis/extra information
    to show writer does not agree/it is mother's opinion

14. beard lop-sided/at an angle (gloss of "squinty")
    elastic too long/does not fit (gloss of "elastic…stretched too far")

15. *Any two from:*
    shoved her/lifted her up/placed her (on his knee)

16. *Any two from:*
    "(miniature) butcher's tools"/ "whatever they were for"/"(little pink) cutlery set"

17. *Any two from:*
    ref to uncertainty ("Whatever they were for")/
    positive reaction ("lovely")/
    could not believe she was allowed to keep it ("It took…mine")

18. high up/looking down/above the lights and bells

19. nothing was bought (apart from food)/they had come for the lights (not to buy things)

20. *Any two from:*
    ref to "natural"/number/movement/sound

21. *Any two from:*
    mother had to pull her away/ref to "All the way back"/sister was right or would not have imagined it/ref to magic

22. gloves were dirty
    experience of the birds

23. (still) feeds birds at Christmas
    first thing

24. If "Yes" suitable ref eg words or actions of sister or mother/ child's reaction to train journey or station or store or Santa or birds
    If "No" suitable ref eg unlikely small child more excited by birds than Christmas toys/Santa

ENGLISH FOUNDATION
READING 2012

1. '(past) midnight'/in bed/asleep
(lift or gloss acceptable)

2. *Any two from:*
crying/screaming/sobs/frenzied

3. *Any two from:*
'still in pyjamas'/'grab'/'rush'

4. *Any three from:*
  (i) (in) schoolbags
  (ii) (in) cupboards
  (iii) (under) beds

5. cool in summer/hot weather
warm during winter/cold weather

6. *Any two from:*
rain/muddy (track)/steering with one hand **or** holding mobile
phone/listening to Sanele

7. 'perilously (close)'/'fatal (mistake)'/'deadly (accuracy)'/'close
enough to kill you'

8. *Any two from:*
do not attack/do not get too close/stay still/'keep calm'

9. see
(lift or gloss acceptable)

10. threat/sudden movement
(lift or gloss acceptable)

11. it is not (all) black/it is brown/olive/grey
(lift or gloss acceptable)

12. opens its jaws/mouth to show (bold) colour/warning (to keep
distance)(s)
(lift or gloss acceptable)

13. *Any three from:*
  (i) lifts head (off the ground)
  (ii) flattens neck (into slight hood)
  (iii) hisses
(lift or gloss acceptable)

14.

	True	False	Cannot Tell
Black mambas try to escape quickly if disturbed.	✓		
Black mambas stare at prey to hypnotise them.		✓	
Black mambas are aggressive if defending young.			✓
Black mambas are faster than people on horses.		✓	

15. create a bank of anti-venom for treating snake bite victims/in
two places/accessible to everyone/accessible within two hours
OR quickly
(lift or gloss acceptable)

16. not (very) painful
little/no swelling
(lift or gloss acceptable)

17. *Any two from:*
'(first symptoms are felt) within fifteen minutes'/'breathing
difficulties develop rapidly'/'death within a few hours'/'two
drops of venom are fatal'/one bite can contain ten times fatal
dose/'enough venom to kill up to 14 adult humans'
(lift or gloss acceptable)

18. dense fields (of sugar cane and maize)/full of prey
(lift or gloss acceptable)

19. 'not easily available'
'expensive'/'locals can't afford it'
(lift or gloss acceptable)

20. *Any two from:*
frantic/drag/pushed

21. short/beginning of paragraph

22.

Snakes can be dangerous and should be treated carefully	✓

any appropriate evidence ie ref. to danger **or** caution
(lift or gloss acceptable)

ENGLISH GENERAL READING 2012

1. walking them/tiring them out/ref. to conversations with people (lifts acceptable)

2. gloss of 'want proper walks' eg need more exercise
   gloss of 'want sticks thrown' eg need to be entertained

3. informal/chatty/colloquial etc

4. *Any two from:*
   ref. to friendly/good-natured/calm/lying down
   or asleep/unobtrusive/no trouble

5. *Any three from:*
   runs riot/eats crisps people have dropped
   sneaks into a neighbour's room/sniffs luggage (for food)
   (lift or gloss acceptable)

6. No ✔
   '(they) laugh'/'(You're a) lovable (chap)'

7. Wilf   sleeps soundly
   Owner   difficulty sleeping/disturbed sleep/anxious

8. ref. to limited daylight

9. ref. to stock-training
   ref. to Wilf's being small
   (lift or gloss acceptable)

10. 'bounding'/'(as if he's) on springs'
    appropriate explanation eg full of energy/happy/excited/
    appropriate ref. to movement

11. *Any three from:*
    beautiful (building)/location/kitchen equipment
    foam mattresses/well swept
    (lift or gloss acceptable)

12. shop is closed
    'breakfast and lunch will finish food supplies'
    (lift or gloss acceptable)

13. 'old slate-mine workings'/'industrial history
    V. 'wind farms'

14. gloss of 'tired but happy' eg contented/looking forward (to meal)
    gloss of 'hopes are dashed' eg disappointment

15. *Any two from:*
    basic kitchen/(black) plastic on mattresses/
    no heating (lift or gloss acceptable)

16. (*a*) it is dog food/Wilf will not share
    (*b*) ref. to phone difficulty
         ref. to expense of taxi

17. alliteration

18. *Any three from:*
    clouds/sunlight
    snow/whiteout
    (lift or gloss acceptable)

19. Word choice   'horror'
    Sentence structure   parenthesis/short sentence
    Climax

20. Cautious ✔

21. *Any two from:*
    'rising wind'/ **or** 'cold wind'/'driving snow into our faces' **or**
    'icy snow' or 'snow into our faces'/rerouting
    'bridge being washed away'

22. proud/feeling positive
    ref to 'He was a breed'/comments of passer by

23. Candidates may approach this question in one of two ways ie, they may separate the achievements of family and Wilf (in which case an example must be given) **or** treat them as a shared experience. In either case ref. should be made to any two of challenges/rite of passage/distance/height/fell terriers

24. To describe the challenges they faced on their trip. ✔
    ref to appropriate evidence eg Weather/anecdotes about Wilf/ difficulties encountered/miles covered

ENGLISH WRITING—2008 TO 2012

	Credit	General	Foundation
	The work displays some distinction in ideas, construction and language. This is shown by a detailed attention to the purposes of the writing task; by qualities such as knowledge, insight, imagination; and by development that is sustained. Vocabulary, paragraphing and sentence construction are accurate and varied.	The work shows a general awareness of the purposes of the writing task. It has a number of appropriate ideas and evidence of structure. Vocabulary is on the whole accurate, but lacks variety.	The work shows a few signs of appropriateness and commitment to the purposes of the writing task.
As the task requires the candidate can	convey information, selecting and highlighting what is most significant;	convey information in some kind of sequence;	convey simple information;
	marshall ideas and evidence in support of an argument; these ideas have depth and some complexity; he/she is capable of objectivity, generalisation and evaluation;	order and present ideas and opinions with an attempt at reasoning;	present ideas and opinions in concrete personal terms;
	give a succinct account of a personal experience: the writing has insight and self-awareness;	give a reasonably clear account of a personal experience with some sense of involvement;	convey the gist of a personal experience;
	express personal feelings and reactions sensitively;	express personal feelings and reactions with some attempt to go beyond bald statement;	make a bald statement of personal feelings or reactions;
	display some skills in using the conventions of a chosen literary form, and in manipulating language to achieve particular effects.	use some of the more obvious conventions of a chosen literary form, and occasionally use language to achieve particular effects.	display a rudimentary awareness of the more obvious conventions of a chosen literary form, and occasionally attempt to use language to achieve particular effects.

A combination of these qualities may be called for by any one writing task.

	Credit	General	Foundation
Intelligibility and Correctness	Writing which the candidate submits as finished work communicates meaning clearly at a first reading. Sentence construction is accurate and formal errors will not be significant.	Writing which the candidate submits as finished work communicates meaning at first reading. There are some lapses in punctuation, spelling and sentence construction.	Writing which the candidate submits as finished work communicates meaning largely at first reading: however, some further reading is necessary because of obtrusive formal errors and/or structural weaknesses, including inaccurate sentence construction and poor vocabulary.

Length	When it is appropriate to do so, the candidate can sustain the quality of writing at some length. Pieces of extended writing submitted in the folio of coursework should not normally exceed 800 words in length. The overriding consideration is, however, that the length should be appropriate to the purposes of the writing task.	Length is appropriate to the purposes of the writing task.	100 words is to be taken as a rough guide to the minimum length expected for each finished piece of work, but the overriding consideration should be that the length is appropriate to the purposes of the writing task.

	Grade 1	Grade 2	Grade 3	Grade 4	Grade 5	Grade 6
Differentiating Factors	The finished communication is not only clear; it is also stylish. Attention to purpose is not only detailed; it is also sensitive. Writing shows overall distinction in ideas, construction and language. Vocabulary is apt and extensive, and paragraphing and sentence construction are skilful. In these respects performance transcends the level of accuracy and variety acceptable at grade 2.	Evidence of one or more of the qualities of distinction in ideas, construction or language is present but these qualities are less well sustained and/or combined than at grade 1. In the main writing is substantial, accurate and relevant, but it lacks the insight, economy and style which characterises achievement at grade 1.	Writing is characterised by overall adequacy of communication. It conveys its meaning clearly and sentence construction and paragraphing are on the whole accurate. There is a reasonably sustained attention to purpose, and structure shows some coherence. Where appropriate there is a measure of generalisation and objectivity in reasoning.	Writing approaches the qualities of adequacy required for grade 3 but is clearly seen to be impaired in one of the following ways: there are significant inaccuracies in sentence construction or the work is thin in appropriate ideas or the work is weak in structure.	Writing rises a little above basic intelligibility and rudimentary attention to purpose. Formal errors and weaknesses are obtrusive but not as numerous as at grade 6. Attention to the purposes of the writing task is weak but the quality of the writer's ideas is perceptibly stronger than at grade 6.	Writing contains many formal errors and structural weaknesses but they do not overall have the effect of baffling the reader. The conveying of simple information is marked by obscurities and extraneous detail, and the presentation of ideas, opinions and personal experience is somewhat rambling and disjointed.

ENGLISH WRITING — 2008

Narrative Numbers 1, 7, 9, 12, 16, 20.

Task specifications/rubric/purposes

The criteria demand appropriate ideas and evidence of structure which in the narrative genre involve **plot** or **content** or **atmosphere.**

Note that the development of setting and character as well as plot is an explicit requirement for all of the short story options.

No 1 *Short story:* imposed opening should be continued.

No 7 *Short story:* imposed title **The School Gate** should be reflected in the narrative.

No 9 *Short story:* choice of imposed titles from which the candidates must select ONE from either **Seeing is Believing** or **Close Up.** Title selected must be reflected in the narrative.

No 12 *Short story:* imposed opening should be continued.

No 16 *Short story:* choice of imposed title from which candidates must select ONE from either **A New Beginning** or **Touchdown.** Title selected must be reflected in the narrative.

No 20 *Short story:* imposed opening should be continued.

Grade Differentiation

1 : 2 *Grade 1* narrative will show **overall distinction** in IDEAS, CONSTRUCTION and LANGUAGE, and will be both **stylish and skilful,** while *Grade 2* narrative will fall short both in the quality and in the **combination** of skills.

3 : 4 *Grade 3* responses will have an **appropriate plot,** will make use of appropriate **register** to create ATMOSPHERE or SUSPENSE and should include NARRATIVE or DESCRIPTIVE details to establish the main lines of the plot. Do not forget that lack of variety in plot and language skills is typical of *Grade 3.* Accuracy is the criterion to establish here.

Grade 4's **simple plot** will approach the adequacy of *Grade 3* but may be poorly organised or have significant inaccuracies.

5 : 6 *Grade 5*'s **very basic plot** will occasionally try to achieve particular effects, and it will also be poorly organised and have significant inaccuracies.

Grade 6 will have a combination of negative features, will be **rambling,** or have **obscurities** in the plot and the marker will have difficulty in decoding because of very poor spelling, sentencing, or handwriting.

NB If candidates ignore the rubric in respect of plot or character this may place them in *Grade 5* in terms of purpose ('few signs of appropriateness'), unless there are other strong compensating features ('accurate', 'varied', 'sensitive'). Where there are no strong compensating features, this may tip the balance overall into *Grade 6.*

Discursive/Informative Numbers 2, 5, 10, 13, 15, 18, 19, 21.

Task specifications/rubrics/purposes

The rubrics cover controversial issues which are likely to elicit emotional responses. Objectivity is not required but clear, straightforward presentation of a point of view is required. At all levels, candidates must deal with the specific topics or, as is the case in one of the tasks, use the imposed format to convey information about a specific activity.

No 2 *Agree/disagree or balanced view.* Candidates may choose to deal with the topic from one particular point of view or take a more balanced approach to the topic. Some background knowledge is required. Personal/anecdotal evidence may figure but should be used to support the candidate's argument.

No 5 *Agree/disagree/balanced view.* Personal or anecdotal evidence may very well feature but should follow a line of thought.

No 10 *Agree/disagree/balanced view.* Personal or anecdotal evidence may well feature but should pursue a line of thought.

No 13 *Agree/disagree/balanced.* Personal/anecdotal evidence may be present but this should pursue a line of thought.

No 15 *Agree/disagree/balanced view.* Some background knowledge is required. Personal/anecdotal evidence is likely to be used but it should reinforce the argument.

No 18 *Imposed format of informative article for school magazine.* The purpose here, however, is W1 to convey information. Some latitude may be required in terms of the degree/extent of the anecdotal/personal. This, too, may influence the tone but is acceptable as it is within the parameters of the rubric.

No 19 *Agree/disagree or balanced view.* Personal/anecdotal evidence is very likely to feature in responses to this rubric.

No 21 *Agree/disagree or balanced.* Both facets of education must be covered (inside and outside). A clear line of thought/argument should be presented with supporting evidence. Anecdotal evidence is, again, likely to feature but should be used to pursue a line of thought.

Grade Differentiation – Discursive

1 : 2 *Grade 1* responses will show a **combination of depth, complexity and skilful deployment** of ideas, and will also marshall evidence in support of an argument.

Grade 2 responses will lack this combination of technical skill and confident tone, presenting ideas in a **less developed** or **sustained** manner.

3 : 4 *Grade 3* will attempt an orderly flow of ideas, which may not succeed logically, whereas *Grade 4* will be typically **weak in structure,** or **have thin ideas** or poorly constructed sentences.

5 : 6 *Grade 5* will present ideas and opinions in **concrete, personal terms** which may be anecdotal, but are more than a bald series of unsupported, **disjointed** or **rambling** statements, the hallmarks of *Grade 6.*

Grade Differentiation – Informative

1 : 2 *Grade 1* will convey information in a **clear sequence, selecting and highlighting** what is most significant. *Grade 2* responses will be **less well sustained** in terms of the qualities of distinction in **ideas, construction and language.**

3 : 4 *Grade 3* will convey the relevant information **in some kind of sequence** which may not succeed logically, whereas *Grade 4* will be **weak in structure** or have **thin ideas** or **weak sentence construction.**

5 : 6 *Grade 5* will convey only **simple information.** Formal errors will be obtrusive but the writing will not be marked by the **rambling** and **disjointed** statements which define *Grade 6.*

Personal Experience/Descriptive Numbers 3, 4, 6, 8, 11, 22.

Task specifications/rubric/purposes

Each of the above calls for a personal response; while there are no genre requirements here, content must be specific and appropriate.

No 3   A single occasion is required. The idea of both the 'journey' and the 'unexpected' should be presented although some latitude should be allowed with the latter. Associated thoughts and feelings should be rendered.

No 4   Some latitude is required here. There may be some overlaps across W1 (conveying information) and W3 (conveying feelings and reactions) and possibly even W2 (deploying ideas).

No 6   The rubric restricts the candidate to a single occasion, although a number of scenes may be used to progress the idea of tested loyalty.

No 8   A single occasion is required. The nature of the 'authority' should be interpreted liberally. The evocation of both thoughts and feelings is an explicit requirement of the rubric.

No 11   A single occasion is required. The idea of the value of the lesson is clearly very open. The lesson, however, must be learned from 'an older relative.' Again, thoughts and feelings should be expressed.

No 22   Description of a scene is an explicit requirement of the rubric. Candidates should choose ONE of the two options.

Grade Differentiation

1 : 2   *Grade 1* will be a well crafted, stylish account and will deploy a range of skills to express perceptiveness and self-awareness and to achieve or create effects, while a *Grade 2* account will be soundly constructed and show a **measure of insight** and self-awareness expressed accurately. *Grade 2* may not be succinct but will be **substantial**.

3 : 4   A *Grade 3* response will be reasonably well sustained, with easily grasped structure, and will on the whole be correct but with a certain dull monotony.

           Grade 4 will be structurally weak and thin in ideas but will still **attempt involvement**, **approaching the overall adequacy** of *Grade 3*.

5 : 6   *Grade 5* may have positive features such as a runaway enthusiasm which may detract the stated purpose but it will present the **gist** of the experience without **ramblings** and incoherence which, along with **numerous errors** and near-illegible handwriting are the mark of *Grade 6*.

Free Choice Numbers 14, 17.

Task specification/rubric/purposes

This question calls for the candidate to determine the purpose of the writing and format. It is, therefore, important that the candidate's writing purpose is made clear in the course of the response. Markers should assess according to the appropriate criteria.

No 14   The rubric restricts the candidate to the use of the picture and its associated ideas.

No 17   The rubric restricts the candidate to the use of the picture and its associated ideas.

ENGLISH WRITING — 2009

Narrative Numbers: 3, 7, 11, 14, 16, 21.

Task specifications/rubric/purposes

The criteria demand appropriate ideas and evidence of structure which in the narrative genre involve **plot** or **content** or **atmosphere**.

           Note that the development of setting and character as well as plot is an explicit requirement for all of the short story options.

No 3   short story – imposed opening should be continued. Candidates may choose to adopt the persona of the gargoyle and this is perfectly acceptable.

No 7   short story – imposed title **Against the Odds** must be reflected in the narrative.

No 11   short story – choice of imposed titles from which the candidates must select ONE from either **The Animal Kingdom** or **Animal Magic.** Title selected must be reflected in the narrative.

No 14   short story – imposed opening should be continued.

No 16   short story – imposed title **Trapped in the Forest** must be reflected in the narrative.

No 21   short story – imposed title **Paradise Lost** must be reflected in the narrative.

Grade Differentiation

1 : 2   Grade 1 narrative will show **overall distinction** in IDEAS, CONSTRUCTION and LANGUAGE, and will be both **stylish and skilful**, while Grade 2 narrative will fall short both in the quality and in the **combination** of skills.

3 : 4   Grade 3 responses will have an **appropriate plot**, will make use of appropriate **register** to create ATMOSPHERE or SUSPENSE and should include NARRATIVE or DESCRIPTIVE details to establish the main lines of the plot. Do not forget that lack of variety in plot and language skills is typical of Grade 3. Accuracy is the criterion to establish here.

           Grade 4's **simple plot** will approach the adequacy of Grade 3 but may be poorly organised or have significant inaccuracies.

5 : 6   Grade 5's **very basic plot** will occasionally try to achieve particular effects, and it will also be poorly organised and have significant inaccuracies.

           Grade 6 will have a combination of negative features, will be **rambling**, or have **obscurities** in the plot and the Marker will have difficulty in decoding because of very poor spelling, sentencing, or handwriting.

NB   If candidates ignore the rubric in respect of plot or character this may place them in Grade 5 in terms of purpose ('few signs of appropriateness'), unless there are other strong compensating features ('accurate', 'varied', 'sensitive'). Where there are no strong compensating features, this may tip the balance overall into Grade 6.

Discursive/Informative Numbers 2, 5, 6, 10, 13, 17, 19.

Task specifications/rubrics/purposes

The rubrics cover controversial issues which are likely to elicit emotional responses. Objectivity is not required but clear, straightforward presentation of a point of view is required. At all levels, candidates must deal with the specific topics or, as is the case in one of the tasks, use the imposed format to convey information about a specific activity.

No 2   agree/disagree or balanced view. Candidates may choose to deal with the topic from one particular point of view or take a more balanced approach. Personal/anecdotal evidence may very well figure but should be used to support the candidate's line of argument.

No 5   imposed format of informative article for a magazine although the purpose here is W1 to convey information.

No 6   agree/disagree or balanced view. Personal/anecdotal evidence may feature but this should enhance the argument.

No 10   agree only. Additionally, candidates must adopt the imposed format of the magazine article although the purpose is persuasive/ argumentative. It is also possible that candidates could present the case for more than one group of animals.

No 13   agree/disagree or balanced view. Personal/ anecdotal evidence is very likely to be used but it should reinforce a line of argument.

No 17   agree/disagree or balanced. Again, personal/ anecdotal evidence may well feature but this should be used to support the line of thought adopted by the candidate.

No 19   agree/disagree or balanced view. Personal/anecdotal evidence may feature but this should enhance the argument.

Grade Differentiation – Discursive

1 : 2   Grade 1 responses will show a **combination of depth, complexity and skilful deployment** of ideas, and will also marshall evidence in support of an argument. Grade 2 responses will lack this combination of technical skill and confident tone, presenting ideas in a **less developed** or **sustained** manner.

3 : 4   Grade 3 will attempt an orderly flow of ideas, which may not succeed logically, whereas Grade 4 will be typically **weak in structure**, or **have thin ideas** or poorly constructed sentences.

5 : 6   Grade 5 will present ideas and opinions in **concrete, personal terms** which may be anecdotal, but are more than a bald series of unsupported, **disjointed** or **rambling** statements, the hallmarks of Grade 6.

Grade Differentiation – Informative

1 : 2   Grade 1 will convey information in a **clear sequence**, **selecting and highlighting** what is most significant. Grade 2 responses will be **less well sustained** in terms of the qualities of distinction in **ideas, construction and language**.

3 : 4   Grade 3 will convey the relevant information **in some kind of sequence** which may not succeed logically, whereas Grade 4 will be **weak in structure** or have **thin ideas** or **weak sentence construction.**

5 : 6   Grade 5 will convey only **simple information**. Formal errors will be obtrusive but the writing will not be marked by the **rambling** and **disjointed** statements which define Grade 6.

Personal Experience/Descriptive Numbers: 1, 8, 9, 12, 15, 18, 20.

Task specifications/rubric/purposes

Each of the above calls for a personal response; while there are no genre requirements here, content must be specific and appropriate.

No 1   the rubric restricts the candidate to a single school trip to a city.

No 8   the rubric restricts the candidate to a single sporting occasion when taking part was more important than winning.

No 9   candidates should stress the importance of a pet in their lives, although reference made to more than one pet would still be acceptable.

No 12   candidates must write about a single occasion although they must also describe the struggle to achieve the personal goal. Some latitude should be given here with reference to the ideas of 'struggle' and 'personal'.

No 15   the rubric restricts candidates to a single occasion although this may be spread over time. Candidates should focus on the new skills gained from involvement in an outdoor activity.

No 18   description of a scene is an explicit requirement. Candidates should choose ONE of the options.

No 20   the rubric restricts the candidate to a single occasion although, again, this may be spread over time. Candidates should also focus on how they became positive role models for a friend or a relative.

Grade Differentiation

1 : 2   Grade 1 will be a well crafted, stylish account and will deploy a range of skills to express perceptiveness and self-awareness and to achieve or create effects, while a Grade 2 account will be soundly constructed and show a **measure of insight** and self-awareness expressed accurately. Grade 2 may not be succinct but will be **substantial**.

3 : 4   A Grade 3 response will be reasonably well sustained, with easily grasped structure, and will on the whole be correct but with a certain dull monotony.
Grade 4 will be structurally weak and thin in ideas but will still **attempt involvement, approaching the overall adequacy** of Grade 3.

5 : 6   Grade 5 may have positive features such as a runaway enthusiasm which may detract from the stated purpose but it will present the **gist** of the experience without **ramblings** and **incoherence** which, along with **numerous errors** and near-illegible handwriting are the mark of Grade 6.

Free Choice Numbers: 4.

Task specification/rubric/purposes

This question calls for the candidate to determine the purpose of the writing and format. It is, therefore, important that the candidate's writing purpose is made clear in the course of the response. Markers should assess according to the appropriate criteria.

No 4   the rubric restricts the candidate to the use of the picture and its associated ideas.

ENGLISH WRITING — 2010

Narrative Numbers: 1, 7, 8, 13, 14, 20.
Task specifications/rubric/purposes
The criteria demand appropriate ideas and evidence of structure
which in the narrative genre involve **plot** or **content** or **atmosphere**.

Note that the development of **setting** and **character** as
well as **plot** is an explicit requirement for all of the short
story options.

No 1   *short story* – imposed title, **The Rebel**, must be reflected
in the narrative.

No 7   *short story* – imposed title, **The Smile**, must be reflected
in the narrative.

No 8   *short story* – the imposed opening should be continued.

No 13   *short story* – the imposed opening should be continued.

No 14   *short story* – the imposed opening should be continued.

No 20   *short story* – imposed title, **The Arrival**, must be reflected
in the narrative.

Grade Differentiation

1 : 2   Grade 1 narrative will show **overall distinction** in
IDEAS, CONSTRUCTION and LANGUAGE, and
will be both **stylish and skilful**, while Grade 2 narrative
will fall short both in the quality and in the **combination**
of skills.

3 : 4   Grade 3 responses will have an **appropriate plot**, will
make use of appropriate **register** to create
ATMOSPHERE or SUSPENSE and should include
NARRATIVE or DESCRIPTIVE details to establish the
main lines of the plot. Do not forget that lack of variety in
plot and language skills is typical of Grade 3. Accuracy is
the criterion to establish here.
Grade 4's **simple plot** will approach the adequacy of
Grade 3 but may be poorly organised or have significant
inaccuracies.

5 : 6   Grade 5's **very basic plot** will occasionally try to achieve
particular effects, and it will also be poorly organised and
have significant inaccuracies.
Grade 6 will have a combination of negative features, will
be **rambling**, or have **obscurities** in the plot and the
Marker will have difficulty in decoding because of very
poor spelling, sentencing, or handwriting.

NB   If candidates ignore the rubric in respect of plot or
character this may place them in Grade 5 in terms of
purpose ('few signs of appropriateness'), unless there are
other strong compensating features ('accurate', 'varied',
'sensitive'). Where there are no strong compensating
features, this may tip the balance overall into Grade 6.

Discursive/Informative Numbers 2, 4, 5, 9, 12, 18, 21.
Task specifications/rubrics/purposes
The rubrics cover controversial issues which are likely to elicit
emotional responses. Objectivity is not required but clear,
straightforward presentation of a point of view is required. At all
levels, candidates must deal with the specific topics or, as is the case
in one of the tasks, use the imposed format to convey information
about a specific activity.

No 2   *agree/disagree or balanced view.* Candidates may choose to
deal with the topic from one particular point of view or
take a more balanced approach. Personal/anecdotal
evidence may figure but should be used to support the
candidate's argument.

No 4   *agree/disagree or balanced view.* Personal or anecdotal may
feature but should follow a line of thought.

No 5   *agree/disagree/balanced.* Personal/anecdotal evidence may
be present but this should follow a line of thought.

No 9   *agree/disagree/balanced.* Personal/anecdotal evidence may
be present but this should follow a line of thought.

No 12   imposed format of article for school magazine, although
the purpose is clearly discursive. Candidates must present
the case either for or against the notion of Scottish
independence.

No 18   imposed format of school magazine article although the
genre required straddles description and W1 information.
Note that there is no requirement for candidates to
include thoughts and feelings.

No 21   is a W1 informative piece on the life skills the candidate
would like to learn at school. While three possibilities are
listed, the candidate need not use any of these.

Grade Differentiation – Discursive

1 : 2   *Grade 1* responses will show a **combination of depth,
complexity and skilful deployment** of ideas, and will
also marshall evidence in support of an argument.
Grade 2 responses will lack this combination of technical
skill and confident tone, presenting ideas in a **less
developed** or **sustained** manner.

3 : 4   *Grade 3* will attempt an orderly flow of ideas, which may
not succeed logically, whereas *Grade 4* will be typically
weak in structure, or **have thin ideas** or poorly
constructed sentences.

5 : 6   *Grade 5* will present ideas and opinions in **concrete,
personal terms** which may be anecdotal, but are more
than a bald series of unsupported, **disjointed** or
rambling statements, the hallmarks of *Grade 6*.

Grade Differentiation – Informative

1 : 2   *Grade 1* will convey information in a **clear sequence,
selecting and highlighting** what is most significant.
Grade 2 responses will be **less well sustained** in terms
of the qualities of distinction in **ideas, construction
and language**.

3 : 4   *Grade 3* will convey the relevant information **in some
kind of sequence** which may not succeed logically,
whereas *Grade 4* will be **weak in structure** or have **thin
ideas** or **weak sentence construction**.

5 : 6   *Grade 5* will convey only **simple information**. Formal
errors will be obtrusive but the writing will not be marked
by the **rambling** and **disjointed** statements which define
Grade 6.

**Personal Experience/Descriptive Numbers: 3, 6, 10, 11, 15,
17, 19.**
Task specifications/rubric/purposes
Each of the above calls for a personal response; while there are no
genre requirements here, content must be specific and appropriate.

No 3   the single occasion may be used as a catalyst for a range of
life-changing experiences.

No 6   candidates must write about a single occasion when
breaking a rule was more important than following it.

No 10   the rubric restricts the candidates to a specific fairground
attraction. Description of the place must feature.
Thoughts and feelings should also be included.

No 11   candidates must write about a single occasion and some
latitude may be required on the idea of a Scottish
celebration or festival. Equally, candidates may choose to
write about their involvement in a number of different
aspects of the celebration or festival.

No 15   the rubric restricts to a single occasion although this may
be spread over time. The way in which the candidate felt
second best should be made clear.

No 17   the description of a scene is required from ONE of two
choices.

No 19   candidates must write about a single occasion when they
were given good advice but did not take it.

Grade Differentiation

1 : 2   *Grade 1* will be a well crafted, stylish account and will deploy a range of skills to express perceptiveness and self-awareness and to achieve or create effects, while a Grade 2 account will be soundly constructed and show a **measure of insight** and self-awareness expressed accurately. *Grade 2* may not be succinct but will be substantial.

3 : 4   A *Grade 3* response will be reasonably well sustained, with easily grasped structure, and will on the whole be correct but with a certain dull monotony.
Grade 4 will be structurally weak and thin in ideas but will still **attempt involvement, approaching the overall adequacy** of *Grade 3*.

5 : 6   *Grade 5* may have positive features such as a runaway enthusiasm which may detract from the stated purpose but it will present the *gist* of the experience without **ramblings** and **incoherence** which, along with **numerous errors** and near-illegible handwriting are the mark of *Grade 6*.

Free Choice Number: 16.
Task specification/rubric/purposes

This question calls for the candidate to determine the purpose of the writing and format. It is, therefore, important that the candidate's writing purpose is made clear in the course of the response. Markers should assess according to the appropriate criteria.

No 16   the rubric restricts the candidate to the use of the picture and its associated ideas.

ENGLISH WRITING — 2011

Narrative Numbers: 1, 4, 9, 11, 15, 20.
Task specifications/rubric/purposes

The criteria demand appropriate ideas and evidence which in the narrative genre involve **plot** or **content** or **atmosphere**.
Note that the development of **setting** and **character** as well as **plot** is an explicit requirement for all of the short story options.

No 1   *short story* – imposed opening should be continued.

No 4   *short story* – choice of imposed titles from which the candidates must select ONE from either **Overboard** or **The Boat.** The title selected must be reflected in the narrative.

No 9   *short story* – choice of imposed titles from which the candidates must select ONE from either **The Experiment** or **The Monster**. The title selected must be reflected in the narrative.

No 11   *short story* – imposed opening should be continued.

No 15   *short story* – imposed title **Sunset** must be reflected in the narrative.

No 20   *short story* – imposed title **Escape from the City** must be reflected in the narrative.

Grade Differentiation

1 : 2   *Grade 1* narrative will show **overall distinction** in IDEAS, CONSTRUCTION and LANGUAGE, and will be both **stylish and skilful**, while *Grade 2* narrative will fall short both in the quality and in the **combination** of skills.

3 : 4   *Grade 3* responses will have an **appropriate plot**, will make use of appropriate **register** to create ATMOSPHERE or SUSPENSE and should include NARRATIVE or DESCRIPTIVE details to establish the main lines of the plot. Do not forget that lack of variety in plot and language skills is typical of *Grade 3*. Accuracy is the criterion to establish here.
Grade 4's **simple plot** will approach the adequacy of *Grade 3* but may be poorly organised or have significant inaccuracies.

5 : 6   *Grade 5*'s **very basic plot** will occasionally try to achieve particular effects, and it will also be poorly organised and have significant inaccuracies.
Grade 6 will have a combination of negative features, will be **rambling**, or have **obscurities** in the plot and the Marker will have difficulty in decoding because of very poor spelling, sentencing, or handwriting.

NB   If candidates ignore the rubric in respect of plot or character this may place them in *Grade 5* in terms of purpose ('few signs of appropriateness'), unless there are other strong compensating features ('accurate', 'varied', 'sensitive'). Where there are no strong compensating features, this may tip the balance overall into *Grade 6*.

Discursive/Informative Numbers: 3, 5, 8, 12, 19.
Task specifications/rubrics/purposes

The rubrics cover controversial topics which are likely to elicit emotional responses. Objectivity is not required but clear, straightforward presentation of a point of view is required. At all levels, candidates must deal with the specific topics.

No 3   *agree/disagree or balanced view.* Candidates may choose to deal with the topic from one particular point of view or take a more balanced approach. Personal/anecdotal evidence may well feature but this should be used to progress a line of thought.

No 5   *agree/disagree or balanced view.* Personal/anecdotal evidence may well feature but this should be used to progress a line of thought. Some latitude may be required in the interpretation of the idea of risk.

No 8 *agree/disagree or balanced view.* Personal/anecdotal evidence may well feature but this should be used to reinforce the argument.

No 12 *agree/disagree or balanced view.* Personal/anecdotal evidence may very well feature but, again this should be used to pursue a line of thought.

No 19 *agree/disagree or balanced view.* Personal/anecdotal evidence may very well feature but, again, this should be used to pursue a line of thought. Some latitude may be required in the interpretation of the idea of a city.

Grade Differentiation – Discursive

1 : 2 *Grade 1* responses will show a **combination of depth, complexity and skilful deployment** of ideas, and will also marshall evidence in support of an argument. *Grade 2* responses will lack this combination of technical skill and confident tone, presenting ideas in a **less developed** or **sustained** manner.

3 : 4 *Grade 3* will attempt an orderly flow of ideas, which may not succeed logically, whereas *Grade 4* will be typically **weak in structure**, or **have thin ideas** or poorly constructed sentences.

5 : 6 *Grade 5* will present ideas and opinions in **concrete, personal terms** which may be anecdotal, but are more than a bald series of unsupported, **disjointed** or **rambling** statements, the hallmarks of *Grade 6*.

Grade Differentiation – Informative

1 : 2 *Grade 1* will convey information in a **clear sequence**, **selecting and highlighting** what is most significant. *Grade 2* responses will be **less well sustained** in terms of the qualities of distinction in **ideas, construction and language**.

3 : 4 *Grade 3* will convey the relevant information **in some kind of sequence** which may not succeed logically, whereas *Grade 4* will be **weak in structure** or have **thin ideas** or **weak sentence construction**.

5 : 6 *Grade 5* will convey only **simple information**. Formal errors will be obtrusive but the writing will not be marked by the **rambling** and **disjointed** statements which define *Grade 6*.

Personal Experience/Descriptive Numbers: 2, 6, 10, 13, 14, 17, 18.

No 2 the rubric restricts the candidate to a single occasion when they receive a telephone call giving unwelcoming news.

No 6 candidates must write about a single occasion in which the memorable nature of the boat journey should be conveyed through their feelings and reactions.

No 10 the rubric restricts the candidate to one instance when science or technology had a life changing impact. It should be noted that the distinction between science or technology is not the significant factor here.

No 13 there is no restriction to a single occasion here. There is also the possibility here of some informative writing although candidates are reminded that thoughts and feelings should be rendered.

No 14 the rubric restricts candidates to a single occasion although this may be spread over time. Some latitude in the interpretation of the connotations of 'childhood' may be appropriate.

No 17 description of a scene is an explicit requirement. Candidates should choose ONE of the options.

No 18 description of a local park is an explicit requirement, although markers should exercise latitude over the interpretation of a 'local' park.

Grade Differentiation

1 : 2 *Grade 1* will be a well crafted, stylish account and will deploy a range of skills to express perceptiveness and self-awareness and to achieve or create effects, while a *Grade 2* account will be soundly constructed and show a **measure of insight** and self-awareness expressed accurately. *Grade 2* may not be succinct but will be substantial.

3 : 4 A *Grade 3* response will be reasonably well sustained, with easily grasped structure, and will on the whole be correct but with a certain dull monotony. *Grade 4* will be structurally weak and thin in ideas but will still **attempt involvement, approaching the overall adequacy** of *Grade 3*.

5 : 6 *Grade 5* may have positive features such as a runaway enthusiasm which may detract from the stated purpose but it will present the **gist** of the experience without **ramblings** and **incoherence** which, along with **numerous errors** and near-illegible handwriting are the mark of *Grade 6*.

Free Choice Number: 7, 16.

This question calls for the candidate to determine the purpose of the writing and format. It is, therefore, important that the candidate's writing purpose is made clear in the course of the response. Markers should assess according to the appropriate criteria.

No 7 the rubric restricts the candidate to the use of the picture and its associated ideas.

No 16 the rubric restricts the candidate to the use of the picture and its associated ideas.

ENGLISH WRITING — 2012

Narrative Numbers: 3, 9, 12, 16, 23.
Task specifications/rubric/purposes
The criteria demand appropriate ideas and evidence which in the narrative genre involve **plot** or **content** or **atmosphere**.
Note that the development of **setting** and **character** as well as **plot** is an explicit requirement for all of the short story options.

No 3   *short story* – imposed title **The Treasure Hunt** must be reflected in the narrative.

No 9   *short story* – imposed opening should be continued.

No 12   *short story* – imposed opening should be continued.

No 16   *short story* – imposed title **No Fear** must be reflected in the narrative.

No 23   *short story* – imposed title **The High Life** must be reflected in the narrative.

Grade Differentiation
1 : 2   *Grade 1* narrative will show **overall distinction** in IDEAS, CONSTRUCTION and LANGUAGE, and will be both **stylish and skilful**, while *Grade 2* narrative will fall short both in the quality and in the **combination** of skills.

3 : 4   *Grade 3* responses will have an **appropriate plot**, will make use of appropriate **register** to create ATMOSPHERE or SUSPENSE and should include NARRATIVE or DESCRIPTIVE details to establish the main lines of the plot. Do not forget that lack of variety in plot and language skills is typical of *Grade 3*. Accuracy is the criterion to establish here.
Grade 4's **simple plot** will approach the adequacy of *Grade 3* but may be poorly organised or have significant inaccuracies.

5 : 6   *Grade 5*'s **very basic plot** will occasionally try to achieve particular effects, and it will also be poorly organised and have significant inaccuracies.
Grade 6 will have a combination of negative features, will be **rambling**, or have **obscurities** in the plot and the Marker will have difficulty in decoding because of very poor spelling, sentencing, or handwriting.

NB   If candidates ignore the rubric in respect of plot or character this may place them in *Grade 5* in terms of purpose ('few signs of appropriateness'), unless there are other strong compensating features ('accurate', 'varied', 'sensitive'). Where there are no strong compensating features, this may tip the balance overall into *Grade 6*.

Discursive/Informative Numbers: 1, 5, 7, 10, 13, 15, 18, 20, 22.
Task specifications/rubrics/purposes
The rubrics cover controversial topics which are likely to elicit emotional responses. Objectivity is not required but clear, straightforward presentation of a point of view is required. At all levels, candidates must deal with the specific topics.

No 1   *agree/disagree or balanced view*. Candidates may choose to deal with the topic from one particular point of view or take a more balanced approach. Personal/anecdotal evidence may well feature but this should be used to progress a line of thought.

No 5   *agree/disagree or balanced view*. Personal/anecdotal evidence may very well feature but this should be used to progress a line of thought. It is also possible (and entirely acceptable) that candidates may choose to write from a personal/reflective standpoint.

No 7   *candidates are required to convey information*/describe a visit to a place of historic interest (some latitude might be required in the interpretation of this) through the medium of an article.

No 10   *agree/disagree or balanced view*. Again, personal/anecdotal evidence may well feature but this should be used to reinforce the argument.

No 13   *agree/disagree or balanced view*. Personal/anecdotal evidence may very well feature but, again, this should be used to pursue a line of thought.

No 15   *candidates are required to convey information* about an interesting sport or pastime through the medium of an article. Some latitude might be required in the interpretation of 'interesting,' 'sport,' and 'pastime'.

No 18   *agree/disagree or balanced view*. Personal/anecdotal evidence may feature but, this should be used to pursue a line of thought.

No 20   *agree/disagree or balanced view*. Personal/anecdotal evidence may very well feature but, again this should be used to pursue a line of thought.

No 22   *agree/disagree or balanced view*. Personal/anecdotal evidence may very well feature but, again this should be used to pursue a line of thought.

Grade Differentiation – Discursive
1 : 2   *Grade 1* responses will show a **combination of depth, complexity and skilful deployment** of ideas, and will also marshall evidence in support of an argument.
Grade 2 responses will lack this combination of technical skill and confident tone, presenting ideas in a **less developed** or **sustained** manner.

3 : 4   *Grade 3* will attempt an orderly flow of ideas, which may not succeed logically, whereas *Grade 4* will be typically **weak in structure**, or **have thin ideas** or poorly constructed sentences.

5 : 6   *Grade 5* will present ideas and opinions in **concrete, personal terms** which may be anecdotal, but are more than a bald series of unsupported, **disjointed** or **rambling** statements, the hallmarks of *Grade 6*.

Grade Differentiation – Informative
1 : 2   *Grade 1* will convey information in a **clear sequence, selecting and highlighting** what is most significant.
Grade 2 responses will be **less well sustained** in terms of the qualities of distinction in **ideas, construction and language**.

3 : 4   *Grade 3* will convey the relevant information **in some kind of sequence** which may not succeed logically, whereas *Grade 4* will be **weak in structure** or have **thin ideas** or **weak sentence construction**.

5 : 6   *Grade 5* will convey only **simple information**. Formal errors will be obtrusive but the writing will not be marked by the **rambling** and **disjointed** statements which define *Grade 6*.

Personal Experience/Descriptive Numbers: 2, 4, 6, 8, 11, 17, 19, 21.
No 2   the rubric restricts the candidate to a single occasion when they felt compelled to buy something new. It is possible that there will be an element of the discursive evident if candidates elect to justify or rationalise the process.

No 4   description of the scene suggested by the picture is an explicit requirement.

No 6   the rubric restricts the candidate to one instance when they made a fresh start. In the interpretation of 'fresh start,' some latitude might be required.

No 8   the rubric restricts the candidate to the importance of **musical** performance to them. Note that this rubric will allow for several performances to be addressed.

No 11   the rubric restricts candidates to a single occasion when their school was closed because of the weather. The ensuing events might be spread over time. Note that the idea of unexpected fun is merely a suggestion; it is not absolutely necessary.

No 17   the rubric restricts the candidate to a single occasion when the preparation for a competition was as important as the competition itself. Both sides of the rubric must be addressed.

No 19   description of **ONE** of the two scenes is an explicit requirement.

No 21   the rubric restricts the candidate to the one place in the world they would really like to visit, although it should be noted that this task could cross over into the discursive-giving reasons for the choice.

Grade Differentiation

1 : 2   *Grade 1* will be a well crafted, stylish account and will deploy a range of skills to express perceptiveness and self-awareness and to achieve or create effects, while a *Grade 2* account will be soundly constructed and show a **measure of insight** and self-awareness expressed accurately. *Grade 2* may not be succinct but will be substantial.

3 : 4   A *Grade 3* response will be reasonably well sustained, with easily grasped structure, and will on the whole be correct but with a certain dull monotony.

        Grade 4 will be structurally weak and thin in ideas but will still **attempt involvement, approaching the overall adequacy** of *Grade 3*.

5 : 6   *Grade 5* may have positive features such as a runaway enthusiasm which may detract from the stated purpose but it will present the **gist** of the experience without **ramblings** and **incoherence** which, along with **numerous errors** and near-illegible handwriting are the mark of *Grade 6*.

Free Choice Number: 14.

This question calls for the candidate to determine the purpose of the writing and format. It is, therefore, important that the candidate's writing purpose is made clear in the course of the response. Markers should assess according to the appropriate criteria.

No 14   the rubric restricts the candidate to the use of the picture and its associated ideas.

Hey! I've done it

© 2012 SQA/Bright Red Publishing Ltd, All Rights Reserved
Published by Bright Red Publishing Ltd, 6 Stafford Street, Edinburgh, EH3 7AU
Tel: 0131 220 5804, Fax: 0131 220 6710, enquiries: sales@brightredpublishing.co.uk,
www.brightredpublishing.co.uk

Official SQA answers to 978-1-84948-243-1
2008-2012